Henry Brinklow's

Complaynt of Roderyck Mors,

and

The Lamentacyon of a Christen Agaynst the Cytye of London,

made by Roderigo Mors.

BERLIN: ASHER & CO., 13, UNTER DEN LINDEN.
NEW YORK: C. SCRIBNER & CO.; LEYPOLDT & HOLT.
PHILADELPHIA: J. B. LIPPINCOTT & CO.

Henry Brinklow's
Complaynt of Roderyck Mors,

somtyme a gray fryre, vnto the parliament howse of England his natural cuntry: For the redresse of certen wicked lawes, euel customs, a[n]d cruel decreys,

(ABOUT A.D. 1542)

and

The Lamentacyon of a Christen Agaynst the Cytye of London,

made by Roderigo Mors

(A.D. 1545).

EDITED FROM THE BLACK-LETTER ORIGINALS

BY

J. MEADOWS COWPER, F.R.H.S.,

EDITOR OF 'THE TIMES' WHISTLE,' 'ENGLAND IN HENRY VIII'S TIME,' 'THE SELECT WORKS OF ARCHDEACON CROWLEY,' ETC. ETC.

LONDON:
PUBLISHED FOR THE EARLY ENGLISH TEXT SOCIETY
By KEGAN PAUL, TRENCH, TRÜBNER & CO., LIMITED,
DRYDEN HOUSE, 43, GERRARD STREET, SOHO, W.

OXFORD
UNIVERSITY PRESS

Great Clarendon Street, Oxford OX2 6DP
United Kingdom

Oxford University Press is a department of the University of Oxford.
It furthers the University's objective of excellence in research, scholarship,
and education by publishing worldwide. Oxford is a registered trade mark of
Oxford University Press in the UK and in certain other countries

© The Early English Text Society 1874

The moral rights of the authors have been asserted

Database right Oxford University Press (maker)

First Edition published in 1874
Reprinted 1904, 2001

All rights reserved. No part of this publication may be reproduced,
stored in a retrieval system, or transmitted, in any form or by any means,
without the prior permission in writing of Oxford University Press,
or as expressly permitted by law, or under terms agreed with the appropriate
reprographics rights organization. Enquiries concerning reproduction
outside the scope of the above should be sent to the Rights Department,
Oxford University Press, at the address above

You must not circulate this book in any other form
and you must impose this same condition on any acquirer

Published in the United States of America by Oxford University Press
198 Madison Avenue, New York, NY 10016, United States of America

British Library Cataloguing in Publication Data
Data available

Library of Congress Cataloging in Publication Data
Data available

Extra Series, 22

ISBN 978-0-85-991964-7

INTRODUCTION.

OF Henry Brinklow, the writer of the two Tracts which make up this volume, but scanty memorials remain. All he tells us of himself is that he was sometime a Grey Friar, but whether of the Convent of that name in the City of London, does not appear. Be this as it may, he left the community, became a mercer and citizen of London, married, and died in 1546. All that has been hitherto known of him or of his family is contained in Bale's *Scriptores Britanniæ* (fol. ed. II. 105), and is as follows :—

"Henricus Brinkelow, civis ac mercator Londinensis, homo pius, fideque magis quàm eruditione clarus, mirabili flagrans divinæ veritatis amore, et erga ejus adversarium Antichristum odio, quorundam eruditorum virorum adminiculis edidit, sub nomine Roderici Morsii,

    Ad parliamentum Angliæ,
    Super Londino querimoniam,
    Expostulationem ad clerum,[1]

Quæ omnia impressa vidi. Obiit anno Domini 1546, Londini sepultus."[2]

It now appears that Henry Brinklow was the eldest son of Robert Brinklow, who held, under lease, a small farm or manor in the parish of Kintbury, Berks. Robert Brinklow's will bears date 5th June, 1543, and it was proved on the 14th September following, so that he died in that year, or only three years before his son Henry. Henry, the author of these Tracts, made his will on the 20th June, 1545, and it was proved 24th November, 1546. He left an only son John, who is mentioned in the will of his Grandfather

---

[1] This work seems to be quite lost. See the *Lamentacyon*, pp. 91, 114.
[2] I am indebted to Mr Pyne for this quotation from Bale.

Robert: "To Henry's son John Brynklowe, all my silver spoons." Nothing further is known of this boy, except that he was to inherit, according to the custom of London, one third part of his father's property if he lived to full age.[1]

Henry Brinklow tells us that he was banished from his native country by the cruelty of the bishops because he spoke God's truth; and that might very well have been the case, considering the very strong language in which he clothed "God's truth;"[2] but I am inclined to think that his marriage may have had something to do with it, as he was evidently a man who would prefer banishment to tamely submitting to put away his wife, as did many of his more easy brethren.[3]

From his Will it will be seen that he carried his peculiar notions with him to the grave. Thus he forbade mourning gowns to be worn for him, "nor no multitude of torches and tapers;" and he bequeathed the residue of his personality to his wife "on condition that she wear no worldly fantastical dissembling black gowns for me" —a hint of which the good woman was not slow to take advantage, for it seems probable that she married again very soon after Henry Brinklow's death. He was determined, too, it would seem, that his battle against Antichrist should be carried on after his own tongue and pen were silenced by death; for he left to the "Godly learned men which labour in the Vineyard of the Lord and fight against Antichrist," the sum of five pounds; and the like sum to his neighbours for a dinner at his burial, which, as well as his prohibition of outward signs of mourning, appear to imply that he looked upon his death rather as a matter for joy than sorrow.[4] And no wonder.

[1] For further particulars relating to the Brinklow family, abstracts of wills, &c., the reader is referred to the notes on pp. 121-5, kindly supplied to me by Colonel J. L. Chester, and printed with his permission.
[2] See p. 6. Mr Pyne suggests that this "banishment" was intended to mislead like the assumed names of author, printer, and place, which is not at all unlikely. [3] See p. 64, and Note, p. 130.
[4] Brinklow's sense of honour in reference to the payment of debts is worthy of note. In the 'Complaynt,' p. 14, he says to take the property of a convicted felon is a great robbery, but that is a small thing compared with the fact that the felon's 'credit is not paid.' In his Will he says, "I will my whole credit be paid, although both my wife and my children be left very poor;" so that in him preaching and practice agreed.

In spite of the battle which had been waged against the Church of Rome, and the abuses which existed under that great despoiler, Henry VIII., Brinklow seems to have lived just long enough to see the king wavering between his wish to keep what he had so unrighteously obtained, and his desire to make some recompense to those whose religion he had so ruthlessly persecuted. The Reformer must have been aware of the tendency of public feeling towards the shows and indulgences of the Church, and he must have known equally well that no dependence could be placed in a Royal Head of the Church who could send on the same day[1] three men to be burned in Smithfield for the Gospel, and three others to be hanged at Tyburn for Popery.

Had Brinklow lived a few months longer he might have seen that great procession which, on Whitsun Sunday (June 13, 1546) passed from St Paul's to St Peter's, Cornhill; he might have seen in that long line, besides the children of St Paul's school, all the clerks, priests, parsons, and vicars of every church, in copes, and the choir in the same manner; he might have seen Bishop Bonner carrying the Host under a canopy, and the Lord Mayor in a gown of crimson velvet, the aldermen in scarlet, and all the City Guilds in their best array.[2] He might have seen all this and more; for he might have seen the Church of the Grey Friars re-opened and Mass said at the Altars, after the church had been re-christened "Christ's Church of the foundation of King Henry the Eighth;"[3] and the sights would have so vexed his soul that he might reasonably have wished himself dead, and well out of a world of which the people were so ready to return to what he would deem their "wallowing in the mire."[4]

There is not much to be wondered at in the fact of the great bulk of the people looking back with longing to the times that had passed away; nor is there anything to cause surprise in the bitter disappointment of the advocates of the new faith. The people had had exchanged for them the rude plenty of monastic times for the

---

[1] 30th June, 1540. See Note, p. 127.
[2] *Chron. of the Grey Friars of Lond.*, Camd. Soc. p. 50.   [3] *Ib.* p. 53.
[4] I imagine that Brinklow died about middle age. His father died only three years before him, in 1543, and from certain expressions in Henry's Will it would seem that he had not been very many years married. I may mention here that in all probability the family sprang from Brinklow, Warwickshire. See Camden's *Britannia*.

starvation which of necessity followed the expulsion of the small farmers from their holdings. Those who retained their farms found, instead of the certainty of tenure and low rents of Abbey lands, a merciless demand to know by what right, or by what lease, the farms were held, and their rents increased to such an extent that very few could pay them; and then they were left to choose between a vagabond's life and a felon's death, if they threw up their lands, and want and oppression, if they retained them.

These Tracts, like those by Crowley and others, contain the judgments of men who wrote after 'reform' had commenced; of men who were smarting under the results of the changes they had themselves helped to bring about. No doubt their disappointment was a reality. They had fancied that the Supremacy of the Pope once got rid of, and the Pope's laws once set at nought, England would become the Paradise of the saints. But alas, no! Instead of Pope Clement, they found a far more exacting master in Pope Henry; and instead of the Vatican Decrees they found themselves writhing and dying under that "whip with six strings," the Bloody Statute of the Six Articles.[1] Instead of seeing a kind of Christian Communism following the suppression of the religious houses, and a fair distribution of the property pertaining to them among the indigent of the land, they saw with amazement that the abbey lands fell to the lot of the rich ones among the Royal favourites, while the poor, who had been content to receive their share of the Church's wealth at the Convent gates, were left to die untended and often unpitied.[2]

Men who are sanguine enough to hope to change a nation's religion and course of life by one sweeping act of parliament, must meet with grievous disappointment; and the political zealot, as well

[1] Reprinted on p. 103 of the vol. of *Supplications* belonging to this series.
[2] "I cannot a little rejoice," said the king to his Parliament, "when I consider the perfect trust and sure confidence you have put in me ... for that you ... have committed to mine order and disposition all chantries, colleges, hospitals, and other places specified in a certain act, firmly trusting that I will order them to the glory of God, and the profit of our commonwealth. Surely if I ... should suffer the ministers of the church to decay; or learning, which is so great a jewel, to be minished; or poor and miserable people to be unrelieved; you might say that I ... were no trusty friend to you, nor charitable man to mine even-christened, neither a lover of the public wealth, nor yet one that feared God."—*Foxe*, 8vo, v. p. 534. No one could say the Royal promises were not good.

as the zealot religious, often finds himself landed very far from the place where his zeal led him to believe his goal of happiness lay. And so was it with such reformers as Brinklow. That they were righteously angry at the abominations which surrounded them, I have little doubt;[1] but their intemperate zeal blinded them to the more immediate consequences of the changes they sought to bring about. Their audiences learned a lesson which it was not intended to teach. The Reformers preached the doctrine of disendowment for the benefit and advantage of the poor;[2] and while they preached the rich men listened, and were not slow to see the advantages which might accrue to themselves. The deed was done; and the fat pastures and corn-lands of the Church became the spoil of the rich who "neither feared God nor regarded man"—especially if he were poor. As we look back on it all we see nothing extraordinary in it. It was but natural that the strong should enrich himself without being over anxious about the fate of the weak; just as the poor were quite prepared to improve their own condition, without bestowing too much thought on the probable future of those who were about to be despoiled. The shocking part of it all is, that all this robbery, oppression, and cruelty, took place in the name and on account of religion.

The union existing between various classes of society is so intimate that the virtues or vices of the one must ever exercise a powerful influence upon the other. The common people of a country cannot be sunk in vicious idleness, and the class above them remain blameless. And the converse is equally true—the vices of a luxurious and profligate aristocracy will ever be imitated in the ranks below. I have dealt more fully with these matters before,[3] so

---

[1] Since Crowley's works were sent to press in 1871, I have lived in a country where the free exercise of other religions than the Roman Catholic is prohibited by law. During this residence abroad I have seen many things, and I am sorry to say, that I cannot but believe in the general truthfulness of the charges preferred in the 'Complaynt,' not only against the Church, but against the Law and its administration as well.

[2] Their anxiety for the welfare of the poor was not the sole cause; the hatred that was produced by the pride of the prelates, and the lack of morality amongst the monks, must be taken into the account.

[3] See Preface to *England in Henry VIII.'s Time*, and the Introductions to *Archdeacon Crowley's Works*, and to *The Times' Whistle*.

that there is no need to enter into the vices which pervaded all classes in the sixteenth century. The question of the social condition of the people at that time remains unaltered: Henry Brinklow adds his testimony to that of others who preceded or succeeded him, and the evidence of all only goes to strengthen the opinion, that it was a period in which this country, with its men of indomitable will, struggled, and fought, and suffered, with the determination to come out of it all with the strength, independence, and freedom which we hold so dear. Some few there may be among us who are looking over their shoulders and sighing for a return to those "old paths" which, happily for us, have been so long obliterated. If such there be, let them diligently study the literature, both Catholic and Protestant, of this period—the writings of the men who were actually engaged in that death struggle, either on behalf of that ferocious king, Henry VIII., or on the part of a Church which, having done much good work for mankind, had become, as far as England was concerned, immoral, depraved, ignorant; and had fallen from its high estate.

No two men, perhaps, could have been more unlike to one another than Pole and Brinklow. Pole, the refined, aristocratic, conscientious Churchman, not satisfied with things as they were, and preferring expatriation to purchasing the highest honours the State could bestow at the price of his self-respect, looked calmly and deeply into the diseases which afflicted Church and State, and scrupled not to lay bare their sores that he might suggest a remedy; but with that gentleness of manner and amiability of expression which rarely eradicate the evils that are deplored.[1] Brinklow, on the other hand, though sprung from a well-to-do farmer or yeoman of Berkshire, possessed none of the aristocratic refinement, or tender regard, of Pole; his conscience was never wounded by any qualms; with him, to see an abuse, fancied or real, was sufficient to insure a torrent of invective; and he, while Pole only sought to remedy or to reform in a gentle manner, and with as little damage as possible,

[1] I need hardly say that I consider the 'Dialogue' (*England in Henry VIII.'s Time*) to fairly represent Pole's ideas and opinions before he found it necessary to fly the country, in order to escape the clutches of Henry, who required his aid in his marriage difficulties.

could see nothing but a total rooting up of all abuses, and the outturning of all who countenanced or profited by them. With two such men it can neither be unprofitable nor uninteresting to examine into some of the points which they discussed from such different platforms, and to try to discover whether they agree ; if they do, then may we rest satisfied that the Reformers did not always exaggerate, and were not for ever harping on imaginary wrongs.[1]

The rise in rents was a fruitful source of misery, and became not seldom the subject of much strong language by the writers of the period. Pole ('Dialogue,' p. 175) speaks of a matter observed by few, namely, the enhancing of rents; for, he says, if the farmers pay much rent, and more than is reason, they must needs sell dear: for he that buys dear may sell dear most justly. The 'Complaynt' goes further, and bids us consider what a wickedness is commonly practised and remains unpunished in the inordinate enhancing of rents, and taking of unreasonable fines, every day being worse than other; this being done especially by those to whom the king had given or sold the abbey lands. If it had not been for 'the faith's sake,' he adds, it would have been better for the lands to have remained in the Church's hands, for the Church never enhanced the lands, nor took such cruel fines, as did afterwards the temporal tyrants ('Complaynt,' p. 9). It must have been a bitter confession for a man like Brinklow to make, that a country which professed to have received the Gospel of Christ, should be worse in such matters than it was fifty years before, when there was no law but the Pope's ('Complaynt,' p. 10).

The condition of wards was such that it was hardly likely to escape the careful observation of the writer of the 'Dialogue.' Twice (pp. 114, 185) this subject is referred to, and it is declared that the guardian had such power over his ward that, after bringing him up and managing his lands without responsibility to any one, he had it in his power to marry him to whomsoever he would. No one can wonder that Pole should declare this to be "a plain servitude and injury,

---

[1] The reader who cares to carry out this idea further, might consult Sir Thomas More's *Utopia* and compare the statements contained in that work with the writings of one or more of his contemporaries on the opposite side.

and no guard to be admitted in good policy." In the 'Complaynt' (p. 18) we read of the innumerable inconveniences which arose from the selling of wards for marriage, on account of the goods and lands which they possessed. To this was attributed much of the vice which prevailed most abundantly among noble and rich men, " and in the Pope's shavelings most shamelessly." As this question of the immorality of the clergy comes up more than once in the 'Complaynt,' it will be as well here, once for all, to repeat what is said in the 'Dialogue.' It is only a question asked, but it is very suggestive :—
" What is the difference between the clergy sending their first fruits to Rome and their spending them on whores and harlots and idle lubbers at home ?" (p. 200). Pole receives the question as perfectly natural, and merely replies that, in the latter case, the money was spent in our own country.

The question of first-fruits was another on which our two men were at one. Pole said ('Dialogue,' p. 126) that it was unreasonable to send them to Rome to maintain the pomp and pride of the Pope, and to assist him in causing war and discord among Christian princes. It would be far better, he said later on (p. 200), to distribute these first-fruits among our own poor at home.[1] The king, with his usual zeal for religion, forbade the clergy to pay first-fruits to the Pope, but ordered that they should in future be paid to himself, with the addition that parsons, vicars, and lords should pay also. Brinklow's charity was small where the clergy were concerned, but he could not be blinded to the fact that the new condition was twice as bad as it was when the Pope was paid. His words on the effect these payments had on the nobility are noteworthy, as they go far to explain the frequent allusions which are met with to the numbers of serving men who went to the bad. He says,—And as touching the first-fruits of young lords' lands, every man can see what harm may come thereof. The lord hath ofttimes when he dies three-score servants. Now if his son want the first-fruits of his lands, wherewith shall he find his father's old servants ? He must bid them shift for themselves ; and so they must take standings in Shooter's Hill, in

---

[1] For further information on Annates and First-fruits, see *England in Henry VIII.'s Time*, Preface, clxx—clxxii.

Newmarket Heath, and in Stangate Hole. And so this paying of their first-fruits is the cause of great theft, robbery, and murder. For commonly the great thieves and robbers are the castaway courtiers, or pompous bishops' servants, that have no wages of their masters ('Complaynt,' p. 40).

Brinklow was urgent that the Sacraments should be administered in the mother tongue; that the whole of the Church service should be read out of the Old and New Testament, also in the mother tongue (p. 47); but Pole had been before him even in this also. He declared it an ill custom to celebrate divine service in a tongue which the people did not understand. He went so far as to 'allow' the Lutheran manner of saying service, because it appeared to him to be the true method, and because its fruits were so manifest ('Dialogue,' pp. 135, 136). Again and again Pole expressed his firm belief in the necessity, not only for performing service in English, but also for having the Gospels in English; and as for the errors which arose, he thought they no more ought to be laid to the charge of having the Bible in English, than that men should attribute diseases to meat and drink ('Dialogue,' pp. 134-8, 211—213).[1] In the matter of musical services, too, Pole was no whit behind Brinklow. The latter insisted that we ought to call upon God earnestly and with hearty mourning; not slenderly, not for a face and custom only, as had been hitherto used, to have an unholy Mass of the Holy Ghost rolled up with descant, pricksong, and organs, whereby men's hearts were ravished both from God and from the thought of all they ought to pray for (p. 7). Pole, referring to the singing in churches, called it a fashion more convenient for minstrels than for devout ministers of divine service, and said the words were so strange, and so diversely descanted, that it was more to the pleasure of the ear and vain recreation than to the inward comfort of the heart. Do but think, he added, if Saint Augustine, Jerome, or Ambrose heard our curious descanting and cantering in Churches, what they would say! Surely they would cry out upon them, and drive them out of churches into taverns, comedies, and common plays, and say they were nothing meet to kindle Christian hearts to devotion, and love of celestial things, but

[1] See *Complaynt*, chap. 23, p. 53, on this subject.

rather to stir wanton minds to vain pleasure and worldly pastime ('Dialogue,' pp. 135, 137).

That Brinklow the reformer should be an advocate for the erection of public schools wherein Hebrew, Greek, and Latin should be taught, and in which a certain number of poor children should be educated free of cost, will excite no surprise ('Complaynt,' p. 52). We are so much accustomed to hear and read of 'King Edward's Schools' and 'Queen Elizabeth's Foundations,' that we are apt to forget that these two princes only *gave back* a small part of that which their Royal Father had taken away. It would be well to bear in mind, now and then, that the better men of the old faith, equally with the better men of the new, were also advocates of learning. And Pole was, of course, among them. For the education of the nobility he was prepared to change some of the abbeys into public schools, while for the youth of other classes he would have good schools in which prudent and well-learned masters should teach Latin and Greek. From these schools such as were found apt were to be promoted to the universities. Another suggestion of Pole's, namely, that two or three small schools, having an income of ten pounds a year each, should be united to form one good school under an excellent master, will call to mind what we ourselves are doing more than three centuries after Pole's death. So long does it take to bring about changes the necessity for which is obvious to all! ('Dialogue,' pp. 187, 202, 203.)

In the 'Complaynt' (chap. 9, p. 23) some strong language is used in reference to judges and lawyers, and a little further on (p. 25) we read of suits being prolonged from year to year; of abuses in Common Law, and abuses in Chancery; and that 'the law was ended as a man was friended.' In the 'Dialogue' (p. 86) Pole declared that judges and ministers of the law had little regard to the good and true administration of justice; that if the judge were the friend of him whose cause was before the court, it could not go amiss, but was sure to be ended according to his wish; that (quoting the proverb used afterwards by Brinklow) 'matters were ended as they were friended.' Again (p. 118) Pole declared the law's delays were another fault; and said he could see men's matters hang in suit two, three, or four years, and more, and then not finished ; the which might have been concluded in fewer days, the subject was so clear. So bad was the custom that he thought nothing short of making the advocates, who were responsible for the delays, pay costs and damages to both parties in the suit, would ever remedy the abuse (p. 191). Of the vexation and delay which rose by the removal of causes by writ from one county to another, or from the country to London, Pole (p. 117) and Brinklow (p. 20) were equally aware; and they were equally aware of the mischief which men suffered from the facility with which an accusation could be lodged against an innocent person, and of the irreparable wrong which was done by forfeiting all the property of men convicted of treason, felony, or murder ('Dialogue,' pp. 121, 197 ; 'Complaynt,' pp. 14, 21).

Pole, not less than Brinklow, directed his attention to a possible division of Church property, or perhaps a redistribution of it, and I cannot but think his proposed plan a better one than the sweeping suggestions of Brinklow. Pole had no idea of casting Church property into the king's ever yawning coffers; but Brinklow, knowing, perhaps, the royal inclinations, and wishing to secure his end by tempting the avarice of Henry, did not forget the share which might fall to him. Pole, after suggesting ('Dialogue,' p. 151) that, on the death of a priest, the whole of his property should go to a common fund, partly for the relief of such as had more children than they were able to maintain, and partly as a dowry to poor damsels and virgins, went on to give his opinion as to what should be done with the incomes of the bishops. His plan was to divide their possessions into four parts ; one part towards building or rebuilding the churches of the diocese ; a second part towards maintaining poor youths in study ; a third to poor maidens and "other poverty;" while the remaining fourth part should remain to the bishop's use " to find himself and his household with a mean number convenient to his dignity" (p. 200). Brinklow went much further than this; so far indeed, that the unfortunate " bishops, deans, canons, and chantries," were not considered in the least. His advice was to employ the goods and lands pertaining to these " to God's glory, to the common wealth, and to the help of the poor," as follows :—First, part might be given to the poor, as well to poor maidens' marriages and poor householders, as to the blind, sick, and lame; *unless it be one half of the plate to come to the king's grace* to be coined. And of temporals he advised that *not more than a tenth should go to the king*, that he might have homage. The remainder was to be employed upon poor cities and towns, and poor occupiers at "three per cent. per ann." ('Complaynt,' p. 51). Brinklow's plan of 'disendowment' ought to have found more favour in the Royal breast than Pole's, but it is questionable whether it did, as neither went far enough to satisfy the king's craving for Church property.[1]

I must leave the reader to compare the opinions of Pole and Brinklow on such subjects as import dues and exports; the number, ignorance, and celibacy of the clergy; the pride and selfishness of bishops; the authority of the Pope, and so on. If Brinklow had been acquainted with the opinions of Pole on these and other questions, he might have had a good word for his opponent, although nothing, I presume, would have moderated his iconoclastic zeal. Pole was painfully aware of the weakness and the wickedness which existed within his Church, and of the earthly character of those who occupied the papal throne. He could manfully declare that it was no part of our duty to help to maintain the pomp and pride of the Pope, who had nothing whatever to do with the defence of the Church; and that the magnificence and majesty of the Church stand not in its possessions and its pomp, but in the stability and purity of Christian life ('Dialogue,' p. 126); a sentiment which Christian men might well ponder over now. Reformer though he was, he was but ill fitted to cope with the crying evils in Church and State in his day; he could point out where the disease lay, but he could not apply the knife with that unflinching nerve necessary to cut it out. It was left to sterner natures than his; to men who, instead of courting the religious retirement so dear to him, seemed only to live when they were actively battling with their foes; well knowing that the struggle for most of them would only end in the fires which blazed in Smithfield, even in the reign of that 'reforming' king, Henry VIII.

[1] The subject is again referred to in the *Lamentacyon*, p. 116.

In these brief notes of comparison between the orthodox and heterodox reformers, I have necessarily touched on many of the more important subjects contained in the Complaint to the Parliament of England. Of course many remain, but the reader will not need that I should refer at any length to them. A glance at the table of contents (p. 3) will show the variety of topics which called for improvement or for removal. Nearly the whole of them (allowing for the strong language in which they are exposed) only go to prove that men were greatly oppressed in those days, and that they were times which demand our careful attention; otherwise we may be led to believe that the condition of things was very different from that which really existed.

The *Lamentacyon* had better, perhaps, be left to the careful perusal of the reader, but I hope he will not turn away from it on account of the very violent character of the language employed. Brinklow, as has been shown, was not the man to mince his words, any more than he minced the matters which he judged to be abuses. Strong language and violent remedies he deemed to be absolutely necessary for the correction of the crimes and wrongs which the City of London, as well as the whole country, then suffered. According to him there was scarcely a man whose public or private conduct would bear the light of day, bishops least of all; and none of these, it would appear, had sunk so low in the scale as the Bishops of London. They had become so bad that, unless the Devil himself ('The Father of all bishops') were elected to that See, matters could not possibly be worse (p. 93).

Now I am not prepared to accept, and I suppose few will accept, this as anything but a very exaggerated expression. That the bishops, not only of London, but elsewhere, should look with an evil eye on the men who stigmatized them as grossly idolatrous and immoral, and recommended Henry to deprive them of their riches, is not to be wondered at. Bishops, like ordinary mortals, will bear a good deal until you come to their temporalities, which often seem to have a more intimate connection with the soul than do things spiritual. But Henry's bishops bore the loss of all things without much outcry—merely burning a heretic now and then as His Majesty set them example—and 'conformed' to the whims which he, as Head of the Church, thought fit to promulgate. In short, they showed very few signs that they were prepared to suffer either death or loss of goods, being well persuaded, I suppose, that the great bulk of the people were ready to change as soon as the opportunity should offer itself. This argues a low standard in priests and people alike, but we have little of which the standard was not low at that time, not only of religion, but of morality, of justice, and of almost every Christian grace. To quote, or merely to refer to, what Brinklow says in this Lamentation against 'constituted authorities' is unnecessary. Using his favourite phrase, I need only say, "Read the 'Lamentation,' and there ye shall see;" but I may add that the chief charges brought against the Citizens of London were, that they utterly refused to receive the Bible into their houses; and not only refused to read it for themselves, but would not hear it read, and hated all who endeavoured to live after its precepts: that the aldermen and rich men sided with the bishops in persecuting heretics: that they provided for the dead, but utterly neglected the poor, blind, and lame, who crowded their streets: that, in any distress, they would call upon saints for aid, and style Mary the 'Queen of Heaven,' endeavouring 'to patch and piece' the Redeemer: that they spent their riches immoderately and upon such as had no need: that, while the poor man and his wife were punished without mercy, the alderman, the gentleman, or the rich man, might be guilty of the same crime and go unpunished: that officers were chosen only for their riches, to the utter disregard of their fitness or morality: that London had shed the blood of the righteous, that it deserved a thousand times worse punishment than the Cities of the Plain, and that it was doubtful whether ten righteous men would be found within it, notwithstanding all the preaching it had heard during the fourteen or sixteen years preceding: that pardons were sold in Lombard Street, as horses were in Smithfield, and that men paid for the Sacrament as they paid for twopenny pies in the streets:—a long list of charges, and a bold, to be brought by the simple 'Citizen and Mercer' against the powerful City of London. That the book was placed in the Royal

INTRODUCTION. xix

'Index Prohibitorum Librorum' was only natural;[1] the marvel is that the author was allowed to die quietly in his bed, instead of by the 'Bishop's blessing, a fair fire,' in Smithfield.

Brinklow is another of the many writers whose reforms have taken centuries to bring about, although men were willing enough to acknowledge how necessary they were to the good of the commonwealth. The chapter on 'lords that are parsons and vicars' (p. 32) is an instance in point. This chapter, or a part of it, has been frequently quoted. Dugdale,[2] immediately after the words 'the newe gospel of Ingland,' adds :—" and so the author goes on with sharp admonitions to the Lay-men that feed themselves fat with the tithes of the churches, whiles the soules of the Parishioners suffered great famine for want of a fit Pastor, that is, for want of fit maintenance for him, for without that, he is scarce to be hoped for." On the same fol. it is said that the impropriations held by them (the laymen) were much more than one third of all the Parish Churches in England.[3] White Kennett quotes the same chapter from the 'Complaynt,' prefacing his quotation with the following remarks :[4]—" The King and a great majority of the Two Houses were still zealous for the doctrines of popery, and establish'd the most absurd articles of it. They did indeed in some sense reform the discipline and the revenues of the Church; but this too, not altogether to suppress the usurpations of the Pope and the monks, but rather chiefly to encrease their own secular authority and interest. This was so evident, that a blunt writer of that age [5] made bold to address himself thus to the members of both Houses." And he adds (p. 131) : "The Editors of the *Monasticon Angl.* Tom. I. recited these words as a *Complaint* made to the Parliament not long after the Dissolution, touching the abuses that followed, in the

[1] Foxe, v. 568.
[2] *Monasticon Anglicanum*, fol. 1050, ed. 1655.
[3] Dugdale in a note says : "This Brinklow who made these remarks was a London Merchant, and is put in the List of Learned Writers by Holinshead." I have not traced his reference to Holinshead.
[4] *The Case of Impropriations*, &c., p. 128, ed. 1704.
[5] *Roderic Mors*, as he called himself ; His true Name is said to be *Henry Brinklow*, a Merchant of *London*. Note by Kennett.

Church, through lay men's possession of appropriated churches and tithes. And (say they) it deserves to be seriously thought on by every lay man that now enjoys any of them, especially where the Divine Service is not carefully provided for." [1]

This matter was bad enough in Brinklow's days, but what have we done during the last three hundred years to amend it? How many lay rectors are there now-a-days who receive the great tithes of the parishes while the vicar is left to starve, it may be, on the small tithes, without the power to render that assistance to the poor which surround him, and which they ought to receive from my lord rector, or my lay rector, if they knew, or if they recognized their responsibilities? As for hope of voluntary amendment, I suppose there is little more now than there was then, and that it will never come. Certainly one cannot wonder at cries for disestablishment and disendowment; but these will not cure the evil: it can only be remedied by the lay rectors themselves. When they, and others like them, learn that their privileges carry with them certain responsibilities and duties towards the parishes from which their supplies are drawn, we may look for amendment. Happily there are a few men who are not content to receive only, but who feel it a duty, and with them it is a pleasure, to give.

"That one priest ought to have but one benefice" (p. 48) was another reform which required three centuries to bring about: it has been done in our own time, and so recently, that we can see men, who, as a class, have been the shame of the Church of England, still holding up their heads among us, and still drawing their hundreds of pounds yearly from parishes which they rarely visit. Thanks to recent legislation and public opinion, the next generation may know this only as a bad custom which prevailed among us for three hundred years. The Church of England may have no power to reform itself as a body: it might have been well with her if she had shown any desire for reform at an earlier period, and if her individual members had done what they could to make less harsh the abuses which they might not remedy. Nor in the matter of Law, have we done all that might have been done. We hear

[1] Collier (*Ecc. Hist.* ii. pt. 2, Bk. iv. ed. 1714) also quotes the passage.

still of its delays, of its expensiveness, of its almost endless courts of appeal, especially in matters ecclesiastical. Brinklow lamented that after some sixteen years' preaching people were not better, and " that the body and tail of the Pope " were not banished with his name ; but what would he say if he could read the words of one of the first of living Statesmen, written towards the close of this year of Grace, Liberalism, and Education, 1874 ? "It is certainly a political misfortune that, during the last thirty years, a Church [the Roman Catholic] .... should have acquired an extension of its hold upon the highest classes of this country. The conquests have been chiefly, as might have been expected, among women ; but the number of male converts, or captives .... has not been inconsiderable. There is no doubt, that every one of these secessions is in the nature of a considerable moral and social severance. The breadth of this gap varies, according to varieties of individual character. But it is too commonly a wide one. Too commonly, the spirit of the neophyte is expressed by the words which have become notorious : 'a Catholic first, an Englishman afterwards,' words which properly convey no more than a truism : for every Christian must seek to place his religion even before his country in his inner heart. But very far from a truism in the sense in which we have been led to construe them. We take them to mean that the convert intends, in case of any conflict between the Queen and the Pope, to follow the Pope, and let the Queen shift for herself ; which, happily, she can well do.

" Usually, in this country, a movement in the highest class would raise a presumption of a similar movement in the mass. It is not so here. Rumours have gone about that the proportion of members of the Papal Church to the population has increased, especially in England. But these rumours would seem to be confuted by authentic figures. ...... There is something at the least abnormal in such partial growth, taking effect as it does among the wealthy and noble, while the people cannot be charmed, by any incantation, into the Roman camp. The original Gospel was supposed to be meant especially for the poor ; but the gospel of the nineteenth century from Rome courts another and less modest destination. If the Pope does

not control more souls among us, he certainly controls more acres."[1]
To conclude, then, I would ask, as I have asked before, are we so much better than we were? In many things, yes; none but a fool would deny it. But in others, and they of first importance, I think not much.

J. M. COWPER.

Watling St, Canterbury, January, 1875.

[1] *The Vatican Decrees, &c.* By the Rt Hon. W. E. Gladstone, pp. 28, 29 (1874).

NOTE. The 'Complaynt' was frequently reprinted. The British Museum possesses four copies, one printed at Savoy, no date; from this our copy is taken; and three others all printed at Geneva, one probably in 1545, the other two about 1550. The text has been collated by Miss Lucy Toulmin Smith (to whose assistance I am much indebted) with the Geneva edition printed by Mighel Boys, n. d., Q in fours, and with the edition, same printer, place, n. d., H in eights. The variations marked A in the foot-notes are those of the former; those marked B of the latter. There are very few differences between A and B, the latter following mostly those of A. Bohn's Lowndes gives the date of the Savoy edition as 1536, clearly a mistake, for we have the date of January, 1541-2, in the book itself, as well as references to events which occurred after 1536. On the same authority we are told that a second edition was printed at Geneva in Savoy by Boys circa 1536, and that both editions are in the British Museum and the 2nd in Lambeth Library. There is a copy in the Guildhall Library, London, "Imprynted at Geneva in Savoye by Myghell boys" also. Chap. xxiiij commences with a four-line cap. N inverted. It varies in other particulars and is probably a later edition.

The 'Lamentacyon' is printed from the copy in the Bodleian Library, Oxford. This was printed at 'Nurenbergh' in 1545. It has been collated with the edition 'printed at Jericho in the land of Promes' in 1542—copy in British Museum—and with the copy (no place) printed in 1548, in Lambeth Library, by Miss Smith. Mr Geo. Parker read the proofs with the original.—J. M. C.

THE COM-

PLAYNT OF RODERYCK

Mors, somtyme a gray fryre, vnto the parliament howse of Ingland his natural cuntry: For the redresse of certen wicked lawes, euel customs, a[n]d cruel decreys.

A table wherof thou shalt fynde in the nexte leafe.

Oh lord god, heare my prayer, and dispyse not my complaynt: loke vpon me, and heare me. Psalme. liiij.

THE TABLE.

[leaf 2]

                                                                     [PAGE]

That comon prayers and a sermon owght to be at the begynnyng of all[1] cowncels. The first chap[ter]   [6]

Of enhansing of rentes by land lordes.
                                            The .ij. [chapter]   [9]

Of the forfetting of the londes or goodes of traytours, &ce.
                                            The .iij. chapter.   [14]

Of the inclosing of parkes, forestes, and chases.
                                          The .iiij. [chapter]   [16]

Of sellyng of wardes for maryage, wherof ensueth adultery, which owght to be ponished by death. The .v. [chapter]   [18]

Of the iniuryes done to the comynalty by the kyngs takers, &ce.   The .vi. [chapter]   [19]

Of the suttylty of seruyng of wryttes, &ce.   The vii. chapter   [20]

Of promoters, which may wrongfully troble a man by the lawe of England, and thowgh he be cast, he shall pay no charges, &cet.   The .viij. chapter   [21]

That all iudges and pleaters at the barre may lyue of a stypend, geuen them of the king owt of the abbey londes.   The .ix. [chapter]   [22]

Of the cruelnesse and suttyltes of the augmen'tacyon and and eschcker, &ce.   The .x. [chapter]   [* leaf 2, back] [24]

Of the prolongyng of the lawe, and of certen abuses in the same, &ce.   The .xi. [chapter]   [25]

That kynges and lordes of presons shuld fynd their presoners suffycyent fode at their charge: and of men that haue lyen long in preson, &cete.   The .xij. [chapter]   [27]

[1] A all the, *for* all

4 THE TABLE.

[PAGE]

That men, which be accused for preachyng, shuld not be commytted into their accusers handes. The .xiij. [chapter] [29]

Of lordes that are parsons and vicars. xiiij. [chapter] [32]

Of lordes which are shepardes. xv. [chapter] [37]

Of first frutes, both of benefices and of lordes landes. The .xvi. [chapter] [38]

Of particular tachementes, that all creditors may have pownd and pownd alyke, whan any man falleth in pouerty xvij. [chapter] [41]

That the rulars of the erth ought to sit in their gates, or els in their preuy chamber dores. The .xviij. chapter [42]

A godly admonycyon for the abolysshment of dyuerse abuses; and of the seruyce to be had in the Englyssh tong. The .xix. [chapter] [44]

'That one pryst owght to haue but one benefyce, and one fermer but one ferme. xx. [chapter] [48] [* leaf 3]

Of the inhansing of the custome, which is agaynst the comon welth. xxi. [chapter] [49]

A godly aduysement how to bestowe the goodes and landes of the bysshops, &cetera, after the gospel : with an admonycyon to the rulers, that thei loke better vpon the hospitalles. The .xxij. [chapter] [50]

A lamentacyon, for that the body and tayle of the pope is not banisshed with his name. The .xxiij. chapter [53]

A comparyson betwene the doctryne of the scripture, and of the bisshops of England. The .xxiiij. chapt[ter] [59]

A brefe rehersal, conteynyng the whole somme of the boke. The .xxv. [chapter] [73]

O MERCYFVLL FAther, Allmyghty God and euerlastyng, beyng wythowt end or begynnyng, without whom nothyng is, by whom alone all thyngs haue their beyng both in heauyn and erth: To the, in whom only is all[1] ayde, to the only do I crye for ayde, inasmoch as thow hast the hartys of all men in thy handys (yea, euyn of pryncys), that it wyl please the, of thy infynite mercy and for thy Sonnys sake, Iesus Chryst our only Redemer, to send thy Holy Spyryt in to the hartys of all the degreys of men in the Parlament howse; that this my complaynt may receyue fauor in the syght of them that sytte in the Parlament, wherby thyngs nedeful may be redressyd to the glory of thy name, the comodyte of the comon welth, and to the better prouysyon for the poore; which is the thyng that I only seke, as to the, oh Lord, it is not[2] vnknowne. *[* leaf 3, back] Almighty God, to Thee only do I cry for aid; send Thy Spirit into the hearts of the members of Parliament.*

Inasmoch as there is no powr but of God, and whan so euer any persons be greuyd, oppressyd, or ouer yockyd, they must resort vnto the hyer powrys for remedy, whych be ordeynyd of God only for the same cause; and inasmoch as the cowncel of Parlament is the head cowncel of all reamys, for, it beyng done with the consent of the kyng, what lawys so euer be made therby, beyng not agaynst the Word of God, we be bound to obserue them. And though they be agaynst Gods Word, yet may we not bodily resist them with any warre, violence, or insurreccyon, vnder payne of damnacyon. But now, contrary wyse, as we may not *[* leaf 4] When a man is oppressed he must resort unto the higher powers for remedy. We must keep the laws, if they are not against God's laws;*

[1] A all, *added*.   [2] A to, *for* not

6 INTENT OF THIS BOOK.

if they are we must suffer death rather than observe them.

I am banished from my country for speaking the truth.
[* leaf 4, back]

God grant the Council may see all wrongs redressed.

resist the powr of a prynce, euyn so may we not obserue nor walke in hys wyckyd laws, if he make any against Gods Word, but rather to suffer death ; so that we may neyther obserue them, nor yet violently resist them in that case. Well then, inasmoch as the Parlament is of soch powr and strength, although I be a man banysshed my natyue contry, only by the cruelty of the forkyd cappes of Ingland for speakyng Gods truth, yet, seing so many cruel lawes and heuy yockys vpon the showlders of the peple of my natyue contry (specyaly vpon the comons), and agayn consyderyng how lytle the poore be regarded and prouyded for, I can but rekyn my selfe bownd to open and disclose vnto the sayd cowncel of[1] Parlament, part of the forsayd yockys. The euerlyuyng God grant, that thei may be as redy to se them redressyd, as their predecessers were to bryng the peple into[2] such calamyte by the makyng of them ! For the which cause I haue[3] made this litle worke, to cause them to haue instruccyon, that thei may se a reformacyon, whereunto thei be bownd ; and for such causys be thei called to gether of God, and for no partycular or pryuate welth to them seluys, nor yet to the kynges grace.

[leaf 5]

THE FIRST CHAP.

THERE OWGHT TO BE CO-
mon prayers and a sermon, in the beginnyng of any cowncel, and so
long as it contynu-
eth also.

[1] A of the, *for* of   [2] A in, *for* into
[3] haue, *added*.

The first chapter.

IT IS A LAVDABLE thing, that in the begynnyng of any cowncel or assemble, the name of God shuld be called vpon, that he of his mercy will send his Spiryt to sanctifye the hartes of them which beare any auctoryte or stroke in the cowncel or Parlament, that thei agree to such statutes and actes as be to the setting forth of Gods glory, the sanctifyeng of his name, and augmentacyon of his kingdom. For whan we call vpon God for such things, we eyther knowlege, or shuld knowlege, that we haue nede of his helpe, and that we cannot, withowt his assistence, neyther determyne nor yet assent to the determynacyon of any thing that may please God; for if we cowld, what nede we to call vpon hym for any help? And it is certen and vnfallible, that if we knock, seke, and crye dilygently, with[1] ernest and harty petycyons, with true humblenes of our hartes, and withowt dissimulacyon, we shal be hard. Therfore, I say, it is both laudable and necessary, that all cowncels be begon with prayer vnto our mercyful Father, and in our prayers to open vnto hym our necessyties, and to call vpon hym for ayde to rule our hartes wholly to seke his glory. But this must be done ernestly with harty mowrnyng vnto hym; not slenderly, not for a face and custome only, as hath bene hetherto vsed, to haue an vnholy Masse of the Holy Goost rolled vp with descant, pricksong, and organes, wherby mennys hartes be rauysshed cleane both from God, and from the cogytacyon of all such things as thei ought to pray for. Wheras it were more conuenyent, that thei were diligently exhorted and put in mynd, to consyder and ponder, wherevnto thei be called, and what a recknyng God wil requyre of them.

At the opening of an Assembly God should be called upon

to sanctify all hearts to His glory.

[* leaf 5, back]

He is sure to listen to us if we cry with hearty petitions.

Commence all Councils with prayer.

The Mass and music distract men's minds.

[* leaf 6]

---

[1] A with the, *for* with

And, forasmoch as the most part of the lordes and burgesses take it rather for an honowr than for an offyce, wherfor thei shal answer; and for a dignyte, rather than for any burthen, to be cownted of the Parliament or cowncel howse; and neuer ponder nor consyder before, what thinges in the realme be amysse to be reformed by them, it were more necessary, in the stede of the mombled and mynsed¹ Masse (wherby neither God is glorifyed, nor the hearers edifyed), that some honest, well lerned man, such one as wold neyther flater lordes, burgesses, comons, nor kyng, but franckly and frely speake the veryte, shuld be appoynted to preach, not only at the begynnyng of the Parliament, but at the least .iij. tymes euery weke so long as the Parliament endureth; and to stand in the pulpet an howr at the least, and not aboue an howr and an halfe,² and there to tell the lordes and burgesses their dutes, and to open vnto them such abuses as are to³ be reformed in the realme. And let ˙all the lordes and burgesses be bownd to be present at euery sermon, or els to be excluded the Parlament howse. If ye wil seke such ways, than wil the Holy Gost lyght in your cowncel, or els neuer, for all your pyping or singing. And kepe both lordes and burgesses all in one house to gether; for it is not the ryches or autoryte that bringeth wisdom. And what shuld one howse make one act, and another shal breake and disanull the⁴ same? That way is not after the doctrine of the Gospel. But now let us goo to other matters.

---

¹ A misused, *for* mynsed
² A by the space of an whole hour at the least, *for* an hour at—halfe
³ A and ought to, *for* to
⁴ A that, *for* the

The seconde Chapter.

Of inhansing of rentys by land lordes, &ce.

COnsyder yow, what a wickednes is comonly vsed thorow the realme vnponysshed, in the inordinate inhansyng of rentys, and takyng of vnresonable fynys, and euery day worse than other; and euyn of them specially to whom the kyng hath geuen and sold ˙the landys of those impys of Antichrist, Abbays and nonryes: which landys being in their handys, but only for that thei led us in a false fayth (as their companyons the bysshops still doo)— but for the faythes sake, I say (for the which thei were iustly suppressyd), it had bene more profytable, no dowte, for the comon welth, that thei had remayned styll in their handys. For why? thei neuer inhansed their landys, nor toke so cruel fynes as doo our temporal tyrannys.[1] For thei cannot be content to late them at the old price, but rayse them vp dayly, euyn to the cloudys, eyther in the[2] rent or in the fyne, or els both; so that the pore man that laboryth and toyleth vpon it, and is hys slaue, is not able to lyue. And further, if another rich couetos carl, which hath to moch already, will gyue anything more than he that dwellyth vpon it, owt he must, be he neuer so poore; though he shuld become a begger, and after a thefe, and so at length be hanged, by his owtgoing: so lytle is the lawe of loue regarded, oh cruel tyrannys! Yea, it is now a comon ˙vse of the landlordys, for euery tryfyll, euyn for his fryndys pleasure, in case his tenant haue not a lease, he shal put hym owt of his ferme; which thing is both agaynst the law of nature and of charyte also, he being an honest man, payng his rent, and other dutys well and honestly. I think there be no such wicked lawes nor customys in the vnyuersal world

Rents are raised by those to whom the king gave the Abbey lands.

[* leaf 7]

It was better for the poor when the Abbeys held the lands.

The poor man is not able to live—

he may beg, or thieve, or be hanged.

[* leaf 7, back]

Tenants are evicted if they have no lease.

---

[1] A tyrauntes, *for* tyrannys   [2] A the, *added*.

agayne. What a shame is this to the whole realme, that we say we have receyued the Gospel of Christ, and yet is it worse now in this matter than it was ouer fyfty or .iij. score yearys, whan we had but the Popys law, as wicked as it was, for than leassys were not known. And now the latyng and engrossing of them (leassys I meane) is one great cause of the inhansing of rentys; wherfore I pray God these leassys may haue a fall, and come to an end shortly.

Matters are worse than they were fifty or sixty years ago, when we had the Pope's law.

Looke well vpon this, ye Christen burgessys; for this inhansing of rentys is not only against the comon welth, but also, at length, shalbe the chefest decay of the princypal com'modyte of this realme. For why? This inordinate inhansing of rentys, which is sprong vp within fewe yerys past, must nedys make all things deare, as well pertaynyng to the back, as to the belly, to the most gret da*m*mage of all the kyngs subiectys, landyd men only except. Yea, and euyn thei themseluys were more welthyer[1] whan their landys went at the old pryce. For why? Thei bye all things the dearer, and yet the comon welth is robbed therby notwithstonding; as the godly which sekyth his brothers welth as his own, will soone iudge. Howbeit this matter is so farre gone, that there is no remedy to the redresse of it but one, and that is this :—If the kyngs grace, of his goodnesse, wil consyder wherevnto God hath called hym, and for what purpose. A kyng is annoynted, to be a defence vnto the people, that thei be not oppressyd nor oueryocked, but by all godly and polytick meanys to seke the comon welth of hys people ; so if his grace will call down the pryce of his owne landes as thei went ouer fyfty, yea ˙forty yearys, and compell all other landed me*n* to the same, vpon pay*n* of forfetting his whole landys, one part of them to the kyngs grace, another to be employed to the comon

The enhancing of rents will be the decay of the realm,
[* leaf 8]

and make what we wear and what we eat, dear.

There is but one remedy—

the King must reduce his own
[* leaf 8, back]
rents, and compel others to do the same.

---
[1] A welthie, *for* welthyer

welth, and the thyrd to the presenter that can iustyfye the matter, a reformacion may be had, to the singular case and commodyte of the comon welth, and that many wayes. For this being reformed, aboue all other actes shal bryng the cloth of England to a contynuall vent, and all vytellys to a resonable price, that all clothys of other contryes shal stey, whereas Englyssh cloth shal come in place, as in tymys past hath[1] done, which thing old marcha*n*tes and all[2] clothyers can tel. So*m*me will obiect, and say it is a comon welth to bryng the[3] comodyteys of the realme to an high pryce; which I vtterly denye to be a comon welth; for what maketh ryddance or good sale so moch, as whan a comodyte is at a pryce resonable? As afore is sayd, whan Englyssh clothes were sold at a pryce resonable, than all other foren cloth steyd tyl that was sold. But now is Englyssh cloth brought to so high a price, that the cloth of many contres is sold afore Englyssh cloth. And that causeth marchantes to kepe their clothes long vpon their handes, many tymes to their gret damage. I will say further. In case this matter be not wel loked vpon, the soner it will be a gretter decay than is yet perceyued. For cloth will be brought to so high a price, that thei will marre all. Aboue all thyngs beware of extremyte; for that euer sekyth a mischeffe for a remedy. For what with the abundance of woll, that goth owt by licencys and by the staple, fore*n* realmes myxing it with their course wollys, thei make better chepe cloth than Englissh marchantys can sell; yea and better for the price. Whether it be a comon welth to bryng cloth to so high a price or not, first demand of the[4] honest fermer. But I speke not of the extorcyonar, grosser, incloser, or gret shepard, but of the honest pore fermer, whether he lyued not better

This matter being reformed, the English cloth will find a market,

and be preferred to other cloths.

English cloth was not so dear as it now is.

[* leaf 9]

Now our merchants cannot sell it, it is so dear.

Foreigners buy our wool and mix it with theirs.

Didn't the farmer live better

[1] A it hath, *for* hath   [2] A olde, *for* all
[3] A vp the, *for* the; B *omits* up.   [4] A that, *for* the

12   CHOICE OF BURGESSES BAD.   [CH. II.

when he sold his wool cheaper?

whan he sold his wolle at an indiferent and meane price, than he doth now, sellyng it[1] for half as moch

[* leaf 9, back]

Farmer and clothier answer, yea;

more? And I warant yow, if he be none of those destroyers aforsayd, he wil say yea. Than demand the clothyer, if he lyued not better whan he sold his clothys for a[2] resonable price the pack, and his carseys for xxij or xxiij pownd the pack, than he doth now, sellyng them for xxx. pound the pack? And except it be a fewe, which be inordinate rich, and eate owt their

they gained more in one pack then than they now gain in three.

neyhbours, thei wil also say yea; and that thei gayned more in one pack than thei do now in thre. And as for the poore spynner and carder, though thei haue a litle more for their paynes, thei pay doble so moch for all things that goo both to back and belly, and scant can get an howse to put in their headys; or, at least, not able to furnyssh it for their very necessaryes. And thus euery one eatyth owt another. And the only

The cause of all lies in raising of rents.

cause of all these is the inordinate raysing of rentys. It is vnreasonable to se how moch[3] thei be inhansed in maner thorowt the realme; except it be a fewe such, where of the leassys were geuen owt ouer xx. or xxx.

[* leaf 10]

yerys. And the chefe cause of all this be euyn the landlordes; for, as he encreaseth hys rent, so must the fermer the[4] price of his wolle, catel, and all vitels, and lykewise the merchant of his cloth; for els thei could

The lords are the cause of all the dearth, that is in this realm.

not maynteine their lyuyng. And thus I say, the lordes be the only cause of all the dearth in the reame. God grant, that the kynges grace loke wel vpon this matter him self! for it is hard to haue it[5] redressed by[6]

Parliament won't redress the grievances

Parlament, because it pricketh them cheffely which be chosen to be burgessys, for the most part, except thei wold chose their burgessys only for their vertuos liuyng, discrecyon, honest behauor, and other godly qualytes, be he neuer so pore; such as wold his neyhbor shuld

---

[1] A it, *added.*   [2] A a, *added.*   [3] A moch, *added.*
[4] A set the, *for* the   [5] A be, *for* haue it   [6] A by the, *for* by

lyue as himselfe. And wold to God thei wold leaue their old accustomed chosing of burgessys! for whom do thei chose, but such as be rych, or beare some offyce in the contrye &ce.[1], many tymes such as be boasters and braggars?[1] Such haue thei euer hetherto chosen; be he neuer so very a fole, dronkerd, extorcyoner, aduouterer, neuer so couetos and crafty a parson, yet if he be 'rych, beare any offyce, if he be a ioly cracker and bragger in the contry, he must be a burges of the parlament! Alas, how can any such study or geue any godly councel for the comonwelth? But and if any man put forth anything against Christes religyon, or agaynst the comon welth, so that it make for the profyght of Antichristes Knyghtes and temporal rulers of the reame, thei shal be redy to geue their consent with the first. And whether this be true or no, let the actys of fewe yerys past be iudge. Euery man perceyueth, that there is a fawt, and thei be greued, that all things be at so high a price, and some be offended at one degre of men, and some at another; as the merchant at the clothyer, the clothyer at the fermer, the fermer at the landlord, which is most iust of all. In London and other placys ther be many offended with the great price of vitells, but fewe men consider the grownd and orignyal occasyon therof; that it is only by enhansing of rentys, fynes, &ce., that maketh all things dere, which is an vrgent dammage to the com'mon welth.—And tyl ye haue a redresse therin, loke to haue all things[2] more derer, make what actes ye can diuyse to the contrary. As touchyng the kings landes, some say that he enhansyth none; and wether it be tru or not, I cannot tel, but this am I sure off, it is as euyl or worse. For the chancelers and auditors take soch vnreasonable fynes and other brybes, that

unless we choose different men.

If a man is a fool

[* leaf 10, back] *and rich, he is sure to get into parliament.*

Anything contrary to Christ's religion is well received.

Prices are high, and every man blames another.

[* leaf 11]

Some say the King has not raised his rents;

---

[1]–[1] A and can boast and bragge, *for* &ce—braggars
[2] A this, *for* things; B *has* things

but his tenants are robbed.

the tenantys were better pay yerely a greater rent ; for the tenantys are halfe vndone in their incommyng ! Who hath the vantage, God knowyth ; wether the king, or that the officers robbe his grace, and polle and pylle his leage subiectys in his name, which is most lykest.

Of the forfetting of landys or goodys of traytors, felons, or morderers.

The iij. chapter.

A law which deprives the family of a felon of his goods.
[* leaf 11, back]

OH merciful God, what a cruell lawe is this ! how farre wyde from the Gospel, yea from the ˙lawe of nature also, that whan a traytor, a morderer, a felon, or an heretik is condemned and put to death, his wife and childern, his seruants, and all thei whom he is detter vnto,

All are robbed and brought to poverty.

shuld be robbyd for his offence, and brought to extreme pouerty ; that his wife, his childern, or next kynred, shuld not enioye his landys, whan thei consentyd not to his death ! Wherfor, to take the landys and goodes, it is a gret robry ; but yet nothing to this, that his credyte is not payd. For by that meanys he forfettyth vnto the kyng, not only all his own goodys and landys, but also that which is none of his. Oh most wicked lawys, by this cruelty is many an honest man vndone ! Alas, what can the pore wyfe, the childern, the kynsmen, or credytor do witthall, being not

If they are faulty let them be punished,

culpable in the cryme ? Iff any of them be fawty, than let them haue also the lawe, that is death, which recompensyth the cryme. No dowt, the riches of men hath helpyd many an honest man to his death, by the couetosnes of the offycers that ferme such things of

[* leaf 12]

the kyng. To this shal some flat˙teryng hypocrite, to wynne promocyon or lucre (wherein he shal shewe that he louyth his own priuate welth better than the whole comon welth, or discharge of the kynges conscyence), shal¹ obiect, and say :—"It is as necessary to forfett the goodys and landes, as the lyfe; and specialy traytors." And why? "For traytors," will he say, "be many tymes noble men of gret landes; wherfor if hys chyld or kynred shuld enioy his goodys and landys, he myght in processe of tyme, be a traytor also, and so reuenge his fathers deth agaynst the kyng." Another bald reason he will haply alledge also:—"Iff so be² the offender shuld but lose his life only, there wold be many more offenders than there be." For why? "A man consydering that he shall vndoo his wife and childerne, it shal cause hym to eschewe that euyl which he pretendyd." To the which I make answer, what man is he lyuyng, although he loue his wife and chyldern as wel as euer did man, that will passe more, or as moch vpon the worldly goodys of his wiffe, and childerne, as he will doo vpon his own life? I say, no man lyuyng, nor that euer lyued; and thow art a flaterer and a dissembler, which defendyst this cause, or any other lyke, vnder such a pretense. And thow art a stablissher of wicked lawes. And where as thow alledgyst, if the childern and fryndes shuld enioy the goodes and landes, thei myght haply reuenge their fathers death; to that I answere, pray thow to the Lord God, and all true subiectys with the, that he wil gyue grace to the kyng, to walke in his vocacyon, to vse and exercyse his offyce, to lyue in the feare of God, sekyng Gods glory only, settyng forth his blessed Word—and for the comon welth to make and stablissh politick actys, depending of the Scrypture, and to make none but such as may be grownded vpon Gods Word. And than, for my life, though the child and all his kynred with hym, hauyng .xx. thowsand to them, rebell neuer so moch, the kyng shal not nede to feare. For God

The child of a rich traitor might avenge his father's death.

Or, the loss of goods might prevent a man becoming a traitor.

[* leaf 12, back]

If you are afraid of rebellion,

get the King to do his duty,

then he need have no fear;

¹ A shal, *added here and in* B.   ² A so be, *added.*

God will defend him.
[* leaf 13]

Witness the late rising in the North.

will defend hym, and not his owne powr, euyn as he dyd many tymes kyng Dauyd agaynst Saul, as 'it is to reade in the Bokys of the Kynges. And haue we not examples at home? How mercifully dyd God quench the fury of the peple in the tyme of the commocyon in the North? I pray God, that we be not vnthanckful for that delyuerance, and such other. Wherfor, I say, let us pray that the kynges grace may walke as is afore sayd, and he shal not nede to feare all his enemys; for God shal be his rock, shyld, and defender. But contrarywyse, if he cast of the lawe of God, making wicked lawes, and stablisshing them (wherby Gods glory is mynisshed, and the pepyl of God oppressyd); than let hym feare. For if God be determyned to plage hym, though he kyll not only those which be traytors agaynst his grace, but also their childern, kinred, and fryndes thereto, it shal not help hym. For God shal sturre vp the hartys euen of his own fryndes agaynst him: from which thing God defend him!

But if he makes wicked laws, then let him fear.

Of the¹ inclosing of parkys, forestys, chasys, & ce. The iiij. chapt[er].

[leaf 13, back]

Consider the miseries which come of Enclosures.

OH Lord God, that it wold please the to open the earys of the kyng, lordys, and burgessys of the Parlament, that thei may heare the cryeng of the peple, that is made thorow the reame, for the inclosing of parkys, forestys, and chasys, which is no small burden to the comons. How the corne and grasse is destroyed by the dere many tymys, it is to pytyful to heare! It is often sene, that men, ioynyng to the forestys and chasys, haue not repyd half that thei haue sowne, and yet sometyme altogether is destroyed. And what land is your parkys? Be not the most part of them the most batel and frutefull grownd in Ingland? And now

¹ A the, *added*.

CH. IV.] RICH MEN STEWARDS FOR GOD.

it is come to passe by wicked lawys, that if a man kyll one of those beastis which beare the mark of no one pryuate person, but be indifferent for all men, commyng vpon his own ground, deuouryng his corne or grasse, which is his lyffelod; and yet if he kyl them vpon his oune ground, being chase or forest, it is felony, and he shal be hanged for it![1] But what sayth the prophete to the makers of this wick'ed[2] act, and such other lyke? "Woo be vnto you which make wicked lawys," &cete. To wryte of what vnreasonable length and breddyth thei be it is superfluos: the thyng is to manyfest. God grant the king grace, to pul vp a great part of his oune parkys, and to compel his lordes, knyghtys, and gentylmen to pull vp all theirs by the rootys, and to late out the ground to the peple at such a resonable pryce as thei may lyue at their handes. And if thei wil nedys haue some dere for their vayne pleasure, than let them take such heathy, woddy, and moory ground, as is vnfruteful for corne or pasture, so that the common welth be not robbed; and let them make good defence, that their poore neyhbors, ioynyng vnto them, be not deuouryd of their corne and grasse. Thus shuld ye do, for the erth is the poor mannys as wel as the rych. And ye lordys, se that ye abuse not the blessing of the ryches and pour which God hath lent you, and remember, that the erth is the Lordys, and not yours. For ye be but stewardys,[3] and be ye sure[4] that ye shal gyue account vnto the Lord for the bestowyng of your ryches. And to you burgessys, seing such thynges wyl not be reformed, but only by your pour and auctoryte, I say to you, as in the beginnyng:—Consyder whereunto ye be called and for what purpose; not for your oune particular and pryuate welth, nor yet for the kynges, in any thing preiudycyal to the comon welth.

If a man kill a deer he is hanged.

[* leaf 14]

The thing is plain, no need to write about it.

If deer must be kept,

fence them in.

See that you abuse not the blessing of riches.

[* leaf 14, back]

[1] A for it! But, *added*. [2] A wicked, *added*.
[3] A For—stewardys, *added*. [4] A certayn and sure, *for* sure
DRINKLOW.

Of the sellyng of wardys for mariage, wherof ensueth adultery, which owght to be ponysshed by death.

The v. Chapter.

OH mercyful God, what innumerable inconuenyencys come by sellyng of wardys for maryage for lucre of goodys and landys, although the partyes neuer fauor the one the other after thei come to discrecyon, to the great encreasing of the abhomynable vyce of adultery, and of dyuelyssh dyuorcement, which hath of late been moch vsed. Now God 'confound that wicked custome ; for it is to abhomynable, and stynkyth from the erth to heauyn, it is so vyle. What myschefe hath comme of it, it is to well knoun to many men, I nede to wryte no furder therein. But for Christys blode sake, seke a redresse for it ; and consydre, that ye be called to the Parlament for such purposys. And further, ye that be godly burgessys and of Christes congregacyon, consyder that euyn the same God that[1] sayth, "Thou shalt not steale," the[2] same God sayth also, "Thou shalt not commyt aduoutry." He that stealyth is hanged, & why ought not he also to be hangyd that commytteth adultery ? Wel, though that vyce reygnyth most aboundantly in noble and rich men, and in the popys shauelings most shamelesly, which shame to take them honest wyues of their oune, I say to you that be godly lernyd, although it raygne chefely in such parsons, shame ye not, nor feare ye not, to make it felony indifferently to all men. Loke you euer to[3] your offyce wherunto ye be called, and seke to discharge your oun conscyence, 'that ye may gyue a good accounte at the day whan ye shal be reygned at the iudgement seate of God, to receyue iudgement according to your dedys.

[1] A that, *added*.   [2] A that, *for* the   [3] A for, *for* to

Of the iniuryes done to the commvnalty by the kyngs takers, &ce.

The vi. Chapter.

OH my hart is heuy to see the great yocke that is vpon the comons, by the parcyal act of ratyng[1] of vytellys, which is most greuous euyn to the poore sort: which ratys were made whan rentys went at a moch lower pryce; for that which went for .xx. shillyngs than,[2] goyth now for .xl. fyfty, yea iij. pound, and aboue in many placys, as I haue touched in the fyrst chapter. And therby all things must nedys ryse to an high pryce. And yet this, by reason it toucheth the profight of the king and of the higher powers, must stand still in effect, to the most gret dammage of the poore. And if the robry of the puruyers were ˙knoune, which bye iij. tymes asmoch as seruyth the kyng, and selle it agayn to their oun aduantage, thou woldyst say there were no such robry. And this is vsed in all maner of thinges! For if a man haue but a copple of hennys and come to the market with them, if these puruyers mete him, thei shal take them from hym by force, and gyue hym for them what thei lyst. Lykewyse, if a man haue a good dogg or hound, it shal be taken from him without any recompence in the kyngs name, whan the kyng shal neuer see them. Is not this a myserable thyng? What is it lesse than robry? And if the kyngs grace sawe the actys of the most part of his puruyers, I am sure his grace wold cause a great sort of them to be hanged, as thei haue deserued. What a pyllage is it to the pore, that not so moch as the poore butter-wife but she is spoyled, and that which standeth hyr in iij. halpens, shal be taken from hir for .i. peny, dyssh and all! And yet ye shal not haue hir redy mony neyther, but a taly, and somtyme neuer payd.

The poor suffer from the rating of victuals.

[* leaf 16]

The King's Purveyors rob the poor in all things.

If the King saw them he would hang them.

They give only 1d. for 1½d. worth of butter, and then take the dish.

[1] A raysing, *for* ratyng   [2] A that, *for* than

[* leaf 16, back.] Lyke wyse .ij. pens for an henne, ˙that standeth hir in .iiij. and aboue. And further more, what hart doth not *Poor farmers are robbed.* consyder, that euin as men must leaue their plow and haruest to serue the king with their cartys, so is it reason thei shuld haue a resonable wagys. What is .ij. pens for a myle? Consydre ye rulers about the kyng, and ye that wyl be counted godly burgesys in the Par- *They are paid twopence instead of fourpence.* lament. Thei had bene better to haue seruyd the kyng for .ij. pens a myle ouer .iij yerys, than now for .iiij. pens. Oh Lord, open the earys of them that shuld heare and redresse this matter!

Of the suttylty of scruyng of wryttes.
The .vij. chapter.

The serving of writs is an abuse. IT is a wonderos great abuse, being a great troble to all the kyngs subiectes (but specyally to the pore) & gret nede to be redressed, that whan a pore man hath long suyd a gentylman, being a lawer, or a man of any substance or frendshyp in *[* leaf 17]* the courte, or[1] of any suttyl wytt,[2] and ˙hath obteyned iudgement and a fynal end in the comon lawe, and is come to the poynt that he must haue a wrytt to attach the body of his defendant; alas, how many wayes, yea how many gyles and suttylteys be there, to auoyde and *A writ serves only for one shire.* escape the seruyng of the kyngs wrytt. Fyrst, one wrytt may serue but for one shyre; as though the kyng were lord but of one shyre! But I demand, why may not one wrytt serue in all shyres, yea in all placys vnder the kyngs domynyon, whersoeuer he or hys[3] may fynd his defendant? Surely ther is no godly reason why to the contrary, but euyn the only priuate welth *It lasts only one term.* of sotle lawers. And, as farre as I can lerne, one wrytt lasteth but for one terme; and the nexte terme he

---

[1] A or, *added*.   [2] A will, *for* wytt and; B *as above*.
[3] A is, *for* or hys

must be at charge to¹ come vp, or at least to send sometyme iij. or iiij hundreth myle, for another. And why shuld it not stand in his ful strength tyl it be seruyd? No why, but the why aforesayd. Agayne, no man may serue it but the sheryff of the shyre or his man, and so many tymes it is sene, that the sheryff or his man (and some tyme both) playe the false shrewys in geuyng tha party warnyng, to kepe him out of the way, or to goo in to another shyre, tyl the pore man or his frynd be out of the contry, or tyl the date of the writt be exspyred. Alas, why is not euery man a shyryffe in this case, as wel as euery man is a bayly to attache a felon? Sure there is no cause why, but that it is not the profyght of the shyryff, or else that men be not studyos to make lawes for the profyght of the comonwelth. Oh, the innumerabyl wyles, craftys, sotyltes, and delayes that be in the lawe, which the lawyers wil neuer spye, because of their priuate lucres sake; wherby the comon welth is robbed. Thei be almost as euyl as the wicked bisshops and prystes of Antichryst, saue only that thei robbe us but of our temporal goodys, and not of our fayth.

Only the sheriff can serve it,

[* leaf 17, back] for sometimes the sheriff and his man play false.

So the Commonwealth is robbed.

Of promoters, which may wrongfully by the law of Ingland, troble a man, &cet.

The .viij. chapter.

HEare another as euyl as that, or worse. What an vnresonable lawe is this, that it shal be leful for any wicked parson to commense an accyon agaynst any true and² honest man in as false a matter as can be diuysed? And if the case be soch that the kyng haue any enteresse in the matter, or that it anything toucheth

[leaf 18]

One man may commence an action against another wrongfully,

¹ A or to, *for* to. ² A true and, *added.*

and the accuser has to pay his own costs only.

the kings profight, although it be found false by the lawe, and that the lawe passeth with the true honest man, yet the villane promoter shal not only escape ponysshment worthyly deseruyd, but also shal pay no peny to the pore true mans chargys. And why? Because it toucheth the kyngs profyght. As though it were lawful for the king to robbe or troble his subiectys wrongfully! Oh wicked lawes, how crye all the prophetys agaynst them and the makers of them! Wher-

Seek to reform these laws, lest you be partakers in reward with the makers of them.
[* leaf 18, back]

for be ye lernyd, ye men of the Parlament, that ye may set to reforme thes so wicked lawes, lest ye be partakers in reward with the makers of them, lest at length (as the prophete warneth) "the Lord be ‘wrath with yow and plage yow, that ye perissh from the right way," &c. Many lawyers and other wil make obieccyons to this, and say, "It were no reason thei shuld be sewyd, for it is a comon welth, wherfor the kyng shuld pay no chargys." To whom I answer,—As thow art[1] blynd in Gods word, so is this a blynd obieccyon. Admytt that it were a comon welth. If the promoter sue in ryght, and the defendant be cast, no dowt the kyngs part is recoueryd euery peny (if the party be so moch worth); well than, let the gaynes of that which is recoueryd beare the losse of him which is wrongfully sewyd. And this is to be consyderyd, because the promoter payth no charges though he be cast, it is a gret coragyng to hym to troble his neyhbor; for he knoweth the worst is to beare his own charges.

The lawyers will say they ought not to be sued,

and the king ought to pay all charges.

That all iudges and pleaters shuld lyue vpon a stypend, & cetera.

The .ix. Chapter.

[leaf 19]

NOW wold I wissh a thyng wonderos nedeful to the common welth, yet by the way of petycyon

---

[1] At *in orig.*

(although the kyngs grace be bound in conscyence so to doo); that in as moch as his grace is come to gret riches by rentys, in maner innumerable, of the abbay landys deposed (which was ryghtfully done); for which cause, I say, his grace is bound to study some way, that part of the yockys of his subiectes may be eased, as I think no one way better than this: In as moch as men be naturally geuyn to troble one another, and comonly the wydow and fatherles and such as lack riches and fryndes be put euer to the worst, by reason that the rich filleth the purse of the lawyers which the poore is not able to doo, and therfor his cause is not heard; for comonly the lawyer can not vnderstond the matter tyl he fele¹ his mony. For this cause, I say, I wold wissh that such as preach before the kyngs grace and his councellers also wold moue him, by the way of petycyon, to put part of the landes to some godly common welth. As to geue a stipend to all and euery man of law that sytteth as a iudge, or pleatyth at the barre in any of his high cowrtys thorow the reame, that euery one may lyue (according to his office) lyke a lawyer, and not lyke a lord, as thei doo with such goodys as thei haue goten by robbyng the pore. I meane not but that the suters shal pay for writing all things; but for councel or for his pleating to pay nothing. And wrytings also had no lytle nede to be loked vpon; for in diuerse courtes for writing one syde of a shete of paper, in which shal not be past x. or xij. lynys, he wil haue .ij. grotys, whereas .ij. pense were to moch. Wel, to the purpose afore sayd, and that the lawyer shal take no peny of no man: I meane neyther the iudge nor the pleater at the barre, in payne of losyng his right hand and to be banysshed from pleating for euer. Which wil be an occasyon that the pore shal be heard as wel as the rich, & than wold thei discorage men to troble

The king has money arising from Abbey lands; he should ease his subjects.

As lawyers cannot understand a matter till they feel the money,

[* leaf 19, back]
Judges should be paid a stipend,

that they may live like lawyers and not like lords.

Any lawyer taking money should lose his right hand.

¹ A steale, *for* fele

their neyhbours wro*n*gfully; where now thei be maynteyners of discord for their priuate lukers sake, 'which pr[i]uate lucre of the lawyers[1] is a bayght to sett men together by the earys in the lawe.

[* leaf 20]

Of the cruelnesse and suttyltes of the Augme*n*tacyon and Escheker, & cete.
The .x. chapter.

OH that the kings grace knew of the extorcyon, oppressyon and brybery that is vsed in his .ij. courtys; that is to say, of the Augmentacyon and of the[2] Escheker, but specially of the Augme*n*tacyon! There hath bene moch speaking of the paynes of purgatory; but a man were as good, in a maner, to come in to the paynys of hell as in to eyther of those .ij. courtys. For if the kyng haue neuer so lytle enterest, all is ours. So by the suttylty of the lawe for their oun aduantage thei make many tymes the king to robbe[3] his subiectys, and thei robb the kyng agayne. Take for an exemple:[4]—loke vpon the clarkys of eyther of these courtys. At his incomyng he shal bryng in maner nothing but penne and inck, and[5] within a litle space shal ˙purchesse .xx. xl.[6] l. ij. or iij. hundreth Marke a yere! Well, it is a comon sayng a mong the peple:—" Christ, for thy bitter passyo*n*, saue me from the court of the Augmentacyon!" I haue knoune dyuerse which haue spent moch mony in that court, and yet at length thei haue geuyn ouer their matters, and had rather lose all their expensys, than to folow it; so endlesse and so chargeable is that court. And there is such oppressyo*n* and extorsyon in those .ij. courtes, that all the subiectes of the reame (so farre as thei dare) crye out vpon them.

Better be in hell than in the Augmentation or Exchequer Courts.

[* leaf 20, back]

Christ, deliver us from the Court of Augmentation.

---

[1] A sake—lucre, *added here and in* B. [2] A of the, *added*.
[3] Roble *in orig*. [4] A Take—exemple, *added*.
[5] A and, *added*. [6] A pound, *for* ij.; B *as above*.

Of the prolongyng of the lawe, and of certen abuses of the same. The .xi. Chapt[er].

OH Lord God, who loketh for any brefenesse of sutys in the lawe? But men be differyd from tyme to tyme, yea from yere to yere, & drawne out of such a length with prolongacions, and be at such charge, that I know many men which haue geuyn ouer their right, rather than to folow the lawe : so profitable is it to the lawyers, to the gret dammage of the *comonwelth. Yea euyn in the comon lawe be there gret abuses, and amongst many other, this one I note, that the playntyff shal many tymes spend as moch as the matter is worth before the defendant shal make him answer. This no dowt is an vndoyng to the poore and a defense for the rich ; for in so long hangyng, before he can come to any poynt, the rich man weeryth the pore. Cut shorter your processe, for shame, for that myght well be determyned in one terme, which ye doo in .iiij. ! And nowadayes the lawe is ended, as a man is frynded : yea, and euyn in the chansery there are many abuses, and among other this is one, that the defendant shal be sworne vpon a boke, and shal swere falsely, and so it shal be fownd by the cowrt ; and the matter shal passe agaynst hym with the[1] playntyfe, so that the court seyth by their own sentence and iudgement, that he is periured, and yet is there no punysshment for periuring in that case. And why ? All for the profyght of the court ! For if periury were punysshed in that case, as it *shuld be in that and in all other, than shuld the court lose a gret somme of mony in the yeare. For than wold but fewe men so boldly defend wrong causys as thei doo, but wold seke to agree with their playntyfes, and pay their due and make recompense for such iniurys as thei commytt. I dout not, but if

Law suits are prolonged from year to year.

[* leaf 21]

Abuses in Common Law.

"The law is ended as a man is friended."

Abuses in Chancery.

If perjury were punished, the [* leaf 21, back] Court would lose a great sum.

---

[1] B *adds* the

my Lord Chanceler dyd ponder wel this matter, he wold be the first that shuld procure[1] a remedy for[1] it. Another thing also worthy to be loked vpon is this: O Lord, how men be tossed from one court to another! Yea, and that for smal matters, and in manyfest and playne causes, euen vpon a playne obligacyon. This matter is surely nedeful to be loked vpon. Make nor admytt no iudge to sit in any court, onles he be able rightfully to iudge any matter or cause that shal be commensed in that court. And being sufficyent to iudge such causes, what shame is it to remoue it from that court to another, as though the kyng were more strongar or more iuster in one court than in another: which surely is nothing but a bucler and defence for the wicked and rych, to prolong delay, and to wery hym that is in the right. Make no iudgys therfore (I say) but such as be godly-lernyd, and able to iudge betwene man and man. And let all thinges be finysshed in that court where thei be begonne; onlesse men appeale in cause of life and death, or for gret and wayghty matters, which may be brought to one head court of the reame; and to haue no remouyng but to that one court, as it was in Moyses tyme.

Breake down some of your courtys, for ye haue to many, being so fylthyly mynystred! The court of the Marshyalsee, I can neyther thynck, speake, nor write, the slendernesse and vnreasonable chargys of that court. If the kyng knewe what boytrye were there vsed, I think he wold neuer suffer them more to kepe court, or els he wold loke otherwyse vpon it. It is meruel, but only that God is mercyful, that fyre descend not down from heauen & destroye that court and the Augmentacyon!

[1] A see, in, *for* procure, for

That kyngs and lordys of prysons, shuld fynd their prysoners at their charge sufficyent fode, & cetera. The .xij. Chapter. [leaf 22, back]

I See also a pytyful abuse for presoners. Oh Lord God, their lodging is to bad for hoggys, and as for their meate, it is euyl inough for doggys, and yet, the Lord knoweth, thei haue not inough thereof! Consyder, all ye that be kynges and lordys of presons, that inasmoch as ye shut vp any man from his meate, ye be bound to geue him sufficyent fode for a man and not for a dogge. Consydre, that he is thy brother, and the image of Chryst, if he beleue and repent for his wicked dede, whatsoeuer he hath done. And if he offend the lawe, let him haue the lawe (as afore is sayd) acording to the offence. If it be death, than let him dye, and for the tyme that he is in thy preson vse him lyke a Christyan. For to put a man to death vncondemnyd is to commyt murder; and to put a man in preson, and to prouyde no meate for hym, so that he sterue for hungar before he be condemnyd, is no lesse than to put him to death. Wherfor it must nedys folow that thei which put men in preson, and suffer them to dye for hungar, are no lesse than murderers. Furthermore, perchance thy cruelnesse in mynistryng vnto him such euyl lodgyng and worse fare, may cause hym to falle into despayre, and so thou, for not mynistryng vnto him that which thow art bound, mayst be partaker of his desperacyon. Many tymes also true men come in to presons; well, whether he be true or false, yet let hym be vsed lyke a man, and not lyke a beast. In some prisons, though it be but for the plesure of a rular, he shal beare his own chargys, which be so vnreasonable that it is nedeful to be reformyd; for such as be poore prisoners, and for the helth of their body desyer to be in comons, and

Prisoners are lodged like hogs and fed like dogs.

If a man offend the law, let him have the law.

[* leaf 23]

To imprison a man and starve him, is murder.

In some prisons men maintain themselves,

and pay four times as much as the best inn would charge.

to haue a bed, he shal pay .iiij. tymes more for it there, than in the derest inn in Ingland, besyde the charges whan thei be quytt; and yet neyther his fare nor his lodging shal be very gay. It were more conuenyent,

[* leaf 23, back]

·that the kepers of prisons had a stypend appoynted vnto them, than to lyue by pollyng the pore prysoners and to augment their sorow. A nother thyng also commyth to my mynd, which is wonderos nedeful to be loked vpon. There lye in the Marshyalsee dyuers

Men lie in prison years without trial.

pore men; some haue lyen .vi. yea, vij. yeares, comming vp to sue for land, some[1] for more and some for lesse; whether their tytle be good or bad, I knowe not; but by reason their aduersarys be strongar than thei, they haue found the meanes to cast them in preson, & neyther can thei come to their answere, nor knowe what is layd agaynst them, nor yet be suffred to depart preson, but lye there more lyke dogges than men.

Servants are sent to Newgate by their masters.

Yea, and like wise in Newgate there lye seruantes by the comandment of their masters. Alas, what an heuy case is it! It were mete and necessary, and a thing to be ernestly desyeryd, that what so euer he be that imprysoneth any parson withowt a iust cause or due proffes,[2] that he were cast in pryson him-self, so

[* leaf 24]

long as the other partye laye there ·wrongfully; and also to forfet the halfe of his goodes or landys (which as shal be found better of them both) to be diuyded in .ij. partes, the one to the kyng, and the other to the person wrongfully impresoned. This were a good snafful for the tyrannes and oppressers, and yet but rightful and charitable. No dowt euery Alderman of London haue powr, which thei vse often for their plea-

The City Aldermen imprison the poor,

sure, and to accomplissh their tiranny, that thei may cast a pore man in preson for certen dayes. And whan his dayes be expired, he boroweth his brothers auctoryte, and so may goo thorow the .xxiiij. Aldermen.

[1] A for land, some, *added.* [2] A proofe, *for* proffes

Yea, many tymes thei preson men for their fryndes pleasure, though the party haue deserued no such punysshme*n*t. This is a cruel and heuy tyranny, and yet there is no lawe to ponissh it. *but there's no law to punish them.*

That men which be accused for preaching, shuld not be commytted in to their accusars handes. The .xiij. chapter.

WHat[1] reason is it, or what Christen hart wil say that it is right, laudable, or lauful, that whan .ij. men be at any controuersye of a matter of lyfe and death, the one shuld be put in to the handys of the other, as lernyd men haue had in tymes past with bisshops, and yet haue bene put in to their handys as presoners; whereof dyuerse tymes death hath ensued, as there be examples of late dayes? Was not one within these .ij. yerys murderyd i[n] the Bisshop of Wynchesters lodge? And than the[2] matter was forged that he hangyd hymselfe. Haue ye not a lyke example of Hunne also? And it is meruel, that any that is in their custody, is not eyther poysonyd or murderyd, were it not the high prouydence of God to preserue them. Wherfore I say, it is not lauful that any parson that preacheth, teacheth, or wryteth the lawe of the gospel, shuld be put in to the handys of the bysshops with whom thei contend. And why shuld not both partys be put in preson tyl the matter be tryed, as wel as the one? And 'if the bysshops the*m*seluys (acording to ryght) shuld be put in preson as well as those whom thei accuse, vntyl such tyme as the matter were tryed and heard before an indifferent iudge, thei wold not be so hasty in accusyng. Yea, what reson is it that bisshops shuld haue any presons at all, but that all men shuld

[leaf 24, back]

If two men haue a controversy

why should one be imprisoned where he may be murdered, as one was not two years ago by the Bishop of Winchester?

Let both go to prison till their cause is tried.

[* leaf 25]

Why should bishops have prisons at all?

---

[1] A *inserts* a   [2] A that, *for* the

be brought to the kyngs preson? For it is manyfest to all the world, that all shauelings which beare the mark of that abhomynable whore of Babylon (Rome I meane) be not only parcyal, but also in dede the very enemyes of Christ and his members, euyn as were their predecessors, Cayphas and Annas, of Chrystes owne natural body. Bysshops ought no more to be lordys of presons, than was Chryst and his Apostyls, which were often imprysoned, but thei neuer presonyd man: wherfore it is manyfest that thei be agaynst Chryst. Oh ye rulers, why than suffer ye them to haue presons in their houses, where thei torment men most cruelly, and peruert them of their fayth most suttylly, and murder them also? Yet not so secretly but God seyth them, though the world seyth them not. What pestylent courtes haue thei, in which was neuer innocent found; but whan so euer .ij. false knaues shal secretly accuse a man, although he were as ignorant as a chyld of .ij. dayes old, yet must he eyther dye, beare a fagot, or recant, or at least pryuyly beare a fagot of russhes in his chamber as Moore dyd; so that whosoeuer come in to their clawys may not escape quyte, belyke many tymes thei be the accusers them seluys. But what reason, yea what extreme cruelnesse is it, that eyther in that court or any other, any man shuld be condemnyd to death, and haue not the witnessys to come face to face openly in the court, and openly to be sworne? And if the wytnessys be found periured in that case, let them euyn haue the same death that the presoner shuld haue had, if he had bene found gyltye. For who so euer sekyth the death of another wrongfully is worthy to haue the same hymselfe ryghtfully. Wherfore ye that be in auctoryte, loke vpon this nedeful matter, and consyder the wordys of the prophete Dauyd:—" Ye eate vp my pepyl with as litle pyty as men vse to eate breade." Reforme, reforme! though ye wil not for the loue of God, yet for feare that the vengeance of God lyght not vpon those lawe-makers only, but vpon other also, for that cruel lawe that was of late made, that a man shal be condemnyd to most cruel death, and not to be brought in to opyn iustesse, as were the seruantys of God, Barnys, Garet and Iherom, so that he shal not answer for hymselfe. I think there were neuer so cruel lawys made vnder the sonne, as the most part of the lawys that haue bene made within these fewe yearys past. Death, death, euyn for tryfyls, so that thei folow the High Prystys in crucyfyeng Christ, sayng: "Nos habemus legem, and secundum legem nostram debet mori,—we haue a lawe, & by our lawe he ought to dye." This mori, dye, dye, went neuer owt of the pristes mouthys syns that tyme; and now thei haue poysonyd the temporal rulars with the same. Wel, be ye warnyd, and[1] serch the Scriptu'rys (which be agaynst yow) and repent in tyme! And ye that haue bene the autors of such actys, seke to redresse them, for dischargyng of your oun conscience. If ye loue the Lord, folow the example of them which ground all their iustyce vpon Gods word: as in dyuerse cytys in Germany this dyreccyon is taken for those that be heretyckys in dede, as be the[2] Anabaptistys and such other. Their dyreccyon is this:—Thei lay no snarys nor grynnys to catch mennys lyues from them, as doo our forked beare woluys; but in case any heretycke do hold any vngodly opynyon contrary to the Scripture, and so be a teacher or a seducer of the pepyl in their wicked sectys, than shal he be commandyd to come afore the iustyce, wheras shal be certen lernyd men, which shal dispute and open the Scrypturys vnto hym, and fatherly exhort and command hym to leaue it. If he so doo, he is brotherly receyued into the congregacyon frely, and not tost and turmoyled, as our forkyd

Reform these things for fear of God.

See how Barnes, Garret, and Jerom were condemned.

[* leaf 26, back]

Follow the example of Germany in its treatment of heretics.

If an heretic hold any ungodly opinion,

he disputes with learned men.

---

[1] A be ye warnyd and, *added*.   [2] A the, *added*.

dragons doo with Chrystes membrys. And after, if he contynue in his wickyd'nesse, or at the first will obstynately contynue and resyst the manyfest truth, than thei banyssh him their contry or cyty vpon payne of his head. And than if he will wylfully or rebellyosly presume to come in to their contry or town, which he was forbydden, he shal lose hys head as ryght is, because he breakyth the commandment of the temporal powrs, and not for his faythes sake. Neither put thei any man to death for their faythes sake; for fayth is the gift of God only,[1] as witnessyth S. Pawl in the first chapter to the Phylippyans; so that no man can geue another fayth. Now let all men iudge, whether these men or our blody bysshops goo nerest the Scripture.

Of lordes that are parsons and Vicars.
The .xiiij. Chapter.

YE that be lordes and burgessys of the parlament house, I requyre of you, in the name of all my pore brethern, that are Englissh men and membres of Christes body, that ye 'consyder well (as ye wil answere before the face of Almyghty God in the day of iudgement) this abuse, and see it amended. Whan as Antichrist of Rome durst openly, without any vyser walke vp and down thorow out England, he had so great fauor there, and his childern had such crafty wyttes ("for the childern of this world are wyser in their generacyon than the chyldern of lyght") that thei had not only almost goten all the best landes of England into their handes, but also the most part of all the best benyfyces, both[2] parsonages and vicarages, which were for the most part all impropryd vnto them. And whan thei had the gyftes of any not impropred, thei

---

[1] A only, *added*. [2] A both of, *for* both

gaue them vnto their fryndes, of the which always some were lernyd; for the monkes found of their fryndes childern at scole. And though thei were not lernyd, yet thei kept hospytalyte, and helpyd their poore fryndes. And if the personage were improperd, the monkes were bound to deale almesse to the poore and to kepe hospytalyte, as the writings of the gyftes of such personages and landes do playnly declare in these wordes, "In puram elemosinam." And as tochyng the almesse that thei dealt, & the hospitalyte that thei kept, euery man knoweth that many thowsandes were well releuyd of them, and myght haue bene better, if thei had not had so many great mennes horses to fede, and had not bene ouercharged with such idle gentylmen as were neuer out of the abbeys. And if thei had any vicarage in their handes thei set in sometyme some sufficyent vicar (though it were but seldom) to preach and to teach. But now that all the abbeys, with their londes, goodes, and improperd personages, be in temporal me*n*nys handes, I do not heare tell that one halpeny worth of almes or any other profight cometh vnto the peple of those parisshes [1] where such personagys and vicarages be.[1] Your pretence of putting down abbeys was to ame*n*d that was amysse in them. It was far amys, that a gret part of the la*n*des of the abbeys (which were geuyn to bryng vp lernyd men, that myght be preachers afterward, to kepe hospitalyte, & to gyue almesse to the poore) shuld be spent vpon a fewe supersticyos monkes, which gaue not .xl. pownd in almesse, whan thei shuld haue geuen .ij. hundreth. It was amysse, that the monkes shuld haue personages in their handys, and deale but the .xx. part therof to the poore, & preached but ones in a yere to them that payd the tythes of the personages. It was amysse, that thei scarsely among .xx. set not one sufficyent

[1]—[1] A where—be, *added*.

BRINKLOW   3

vicare to preach for the tythes that thei receyued. But see now how it that was amysse is amended, for all the goodly pretense. It is amended, euen as the deuel mendyd his damys legg (as it is in the prouerbe): whan he shuld haue set it right, he bracke it quyte in pecys! The monkes gave to lytle almesse, and set vnable parsons many tymes in their benyfyces. But now, where .xx. pownd was geuen yearly to the poore, in moo than an .C. places in Ingland, is not one meales meate geuen. This is a fayre amendment. Where thei had alweys one or other vicar, that eyther preached or hyred some to preach; now 'is there no vicar at all, but the fermer is vicar and person all to gether, and onely an old cast away monke or fryre, which can scarsely say his mattens, is hyred for .xx. or .xxx. shillings, meat and drinck; yea, in some place, for meate and drinck alone withowt any wages.

I knowe, and not I alone, but .xx. M. moo knowe, more than .v. C. vycarages and personages, thus well and gospelly serued, after the newe gospel of Ingland. And if a man say to the fermers, "Why haue the peple no preachers, seing ye haue the tythes and offrings ye shuld fynd preachers?" Thei will answere, "We have hyred the personages of this or that lord, and he, or he, is person or vicar; we pay for the tythes and offerings to the lord that is parson." Well than, I say vnto the, my lord parson & vicar, thou doyst wrong to haue personages and vicarages, to haue the tenth pyg, the tenth sheefe, the tenth lambe, goose, flese, and so of all other things, seing that thou art no mynyster nor no pryst of Christes church, & canst neyther preach,[1] teach, nor doo any offyce of a 'parson or of a vicar, but polle & pylle! What canst thou say for[2] thy selfe, my lord parson and vicar? Thow wilt say, parauenture, "The kyng gave me the abbey and

---

[1] A &—preach, *added*.   [2] A of, *for* for

all that longeth therto, which had them geuen hym be the parlament. Therfor if thou speake against my being person & vicar, though I neyther preach nor teach, nor yet procure none to do it for me, thou art a traytor; for this is[1] the .xiij. artycle of our crede added of late, that what so euer the parlament doth, must nedys be well done, and the parlament, or any proclamacyon owt of the parlament tyme, cannot erre. Therfor let no man be so hardy in payne of death, to speake or complayne for the redresse of any thing that is done amysse, eyther by the parlament or by any proclamacyon." If this be so, my ord parson, than haue ye brought Rome home to your own dores, & geuen the auctoryte to the kyng and[2] the parlament, that the carnal bisshops gaue vnto the pope; which was this :— " Si papa, &ce." If the pope thorow his faut shuld[3] send infynyte thousandes to the deuyl, ˙yet must no man speake agaynst him! And if ye haue geuen the same auctoryte vnto the parlament, that the papistes gaue to their general councels, that is, that thei can not erre, and whatsoeuer is onys determyned in a general councel must nedys be true, and of no lesse auctoryte than the gospel :—if this be so, it is all in vayne to loke for any amendment of any thing; and we be in as euyl case as whan we were vnder the bisshop of Rome, if we haue all the lawes of hym confyrmed with fyre and death. Surely the popissh bisshops, whan thei were robbed of the pope of Rome, thei wold nedys haue a pope; and therfor thei wold haue made the kyng their pope, and they gaue hym auctoryte to doo all things in England that the pope dyd in Rome; as, to forbyd maryage certen tymes in the yeare, and than to sell licencys for the same; to selle lycence to eate flessh in lent, non-residencys, and such other.[4] And

The king gave us the abbeys and all that belonged thereto.

No man is allowed to complain.

Rome brought to our doors.

[* leaf 30]

If Parliament cannot err, it is vain

to look for amendment.

When the bishops were robbed of the Pope of Rome, they would have made the King pope.

---

[1] A is, *added.*   [2] A to the, *for* the   [3] A shuld, *added.*
[4] A non—other, *added.*

euen¹ the popys proctor sayd (as it was told me²) that he might make sayntes also! And lesse there shuld want anything to a perfyght pope dome, the 'bisshops caused a proclamacyon to be set out in the kyngs name, that from henseforth the ceremonyes of the church, that were of the popys makyng, shuld no more be taken for the popys ceremonys, but the kyngs; and so thei made the kyng father to the popys childern. But I am sure, though the bisshops wold make the kyng pope, he wold not take it vpon hym. And I trust, that every day more and more his grace shal spye their³ popissh intentys. But to yow, my lord personys, how can ye defend yourselvys, if a man shuld bring this argument agaynst you, and proue you all theuys, that haue personages and vicarages in your handes and cannot preach? Christ sayeth, Ihon the .x. "he that entreth not into the shepefold by the dore, but clymeth in another way, is a thefe and a murderer;" but ye entred in another way, wherfore ye are theuys and murderers. That ye come not in by the dore, I wil proue it thus:—Christ is the dore, but by Christ ye came not in to the shepe fold; that is to say,⁴ to be parsons and vicars, for ye grant that ye came ˙in by the act of parlament, and the act of parlament is not Christ, for it is not confirmed by Christes word; therfor ye came not by Christ, and so be ye theuys and murderers; as your workes prouyd of late, in shedding of the blode of so many true prechers and shepardes, which spent their lyues for their shepe. If this argument be not strong inough, what say ye by this? "All they that come before me (sayth Christ) are theuys and robbers;" ye come into the shepefold before Christ; ergo, ye be theuys and robbars. To come in before Christ, is to be a parson or a vicar before Christ send⁵ hym. And ye came in before Christ

The King able to make saints.
[* leaf 30, back]

But the King would not take the office upon him.

My lord parsons are all thieves and murderers;

[* leaf 31]

they shed the blood of many preachers.

---

¹ A euen, *added.* ² A as—me, *added.* ³ A wyly, *after* their
⁴ A to say, *added.*   ⁵ A set, *for* send

sent yow, for he sendeth none to be shepardes, but such as he knoweth to be able to fede his flocke : ergo, he neuer sent yow ; for he knoweth yow vnable to doo that office. And thus to conclude, ye be theues and robbers, for a thefe commeth not but to steale and to kyll. Wherfor gyue ouer your personages to learned men, & enter not in to other mennys vocacyons, to robbe the ministers both of their office & of their ˙liuyng, that ye be not punisshed of God. But if ye will nedys be parsons and vicars styll, and haue all the profightes of the personages, and will haue all, euen to the tythe eg of a pore woman that hath but .ij. hennys, ye must haue the paynes that belong to such parsons as yow be. Heare what Almighty God sayth vnto yow my lordys, which wil be parsons and pastors, Ezechiel .xxxiij :— "If I say vnto the wicked, thou shalt dye the death, and thou speake not vnto hym, to kepe the wicked from his way, the wicked his own selfe shal dye in his wickednes, but his blode shall I requyre of thy hand." Mark well, lord parson, for this is sayd to all them that are parsons, and take wages and liuyng of the peple, as tythes and offryngs, for feding of them with Gods word ; or els by what tytle canst thow chalenge the tythes ? Loke well vpon this matter, and byld thy conscyence vpon Godds word.

[Christ sends none to be shepherds but such as are able to feed His flock.]

[* leaf 31, back]

[The profit and punishment go together.]

[The blood of the wicked will be required at your hands.]

[Look well to this.]

Of lordes which are shepardes.

The .xv. Chapter.

WHan the sprytualty was in prosperyte & had the vpper hand in the reame, thei did farre excede the temporal lordes in couetosnes ; but after thei had a falle, & the lordes hauyng their spoyles, the same pock that was in the clargys wyne and clothes, hath so infected the gentylmen of the temporaltye that thei can not be

[* leaf 32]

[When the laity gained the spoil from the clergy]

they were infected with the same disease.

content with the sufficye*n*t lyuelodes that their fathers left them; but thei wil inhance, not only the rentes of their londes yearly (which thei nede not to do) but also, to get riches, thei wil become parsons, vicars, myllers, masons, and shepardes; so that no ma*n* that was wont to lyue by his shepe, can now haue any pastor for them, by the reason that lordes flockes eate vp the corne, medows, heathes, and all together. Thes

These gentlemen say we keep no order; but what order do they keep?

gentylmen wil say that we wil kepe no ordre, whan we breake a ceremony of the popes making.¹ But I pray yow,² what ordre kepe thei, that neuer toke ordre in their life, and inordynately take the liuyng of the ministers of the church, & thurst the*m*selues in to other me*n*'nys vocacyons? And where as thei shuld be lordes and rulars, thei become parsons & shepardes and marcha*n*tes, so that no man can haue any liuyng for them. It were necessari that this were amended, and that no lord had moo shepe than be able to serue his house; and he that³ doth excede, to forfet his whole flocke, half to the kyng and half to the complayner.

[* leaf 32, back] *Instead of being lords they become parsons and shepherds.*

Of first frutes, both of benifyces and lordes landes. The .xvi. Chapt[er].

As we have denied the Pope,

FOrasmoch as we haue denyed the Popes name, it is conuenient that we also denye all his naughty condycyo*n*s there with, that all the whole⁴ pope, with all popistry, may be vtterly denyed and banysshed. The pope, ex plenitudine potestatis, made a lawe, that euery bisshop shuld lack the first yeare all the frutes of his bisshopryke, though the bisshop were so worthy his liuyng the first yeare as the worthyest of all the Apostels. And he ordeyned that these first frutes shuld neyther ˙be geuen to blynd nor

we should deny papistry.

[* leaf 33]

¹ A making, *added*.   ² A I pray yow, *added*.
³ A he that, *added*; B *omits* that   ⁴ A whole, *added*.

lame, but to himself, to mayntayne his pryde. This
condicyon of the pope is now confirmed in Ingland with *The law of first fruits is now confirmed by Parliament.*
an act of the parlament, wherby not only bisshops must
pay the first frutes of their bisshoprickes, but also euery
parson and vicar of his benyfyce, and euery lord the
first frutes of his landys. In which act the popes condicyon is not put away, but it is .ij. partes gretter than
euer it was. For where the bisshops only did pay the
first frutes than, now the parsons pay, the vicars pay, *It is all pay, pay.*
the lordes pay, and in conclusyon all men must so often
pay, pay, that a man if he toke not good hede wold
thynk, that the Latyn papa were translated in to *"Papa" is translated into "pay pay."*
Englissh; here is so moch payng on euery syde! But
I iudge that the kyngs grace was neuer the cause of
thys payng, but thei whom the vengeance of God both
hath & wil ponissh. Wherfor I thinck if the parlament, which granted the kyng the first frutes, wold re-
store them to the good shepardes agayne, the kyngs
grace could be as wel content to scrape out this vn-
charyta'ble pay, pay, as he was to put out of his[1] [*leaf 33, back*]
reame that Romyssh papa. Specially seing it is cleane
contrary to the word of God, and playn robbry, if men
durst so call it Heare what the Scripture sayth of the
lyuyng of prechers. "Thou shal not mosel the mouth *The Scriptures forbid men to muzzle the ox.*
of the oxe that tredyth out the corne;" that is to say,
he that taketh paynes to expound the Scripture, ought
not to be defrauded of his liuing for his labor. And
seing that God forbad that no day the oxe shuld be
moselled from his meate, he that shuld .ij. dayes mosel
a laboring oxe shuld breake Gods commandment mani- *If a man did this he broke God's law;*
festly. And he that shuld mosel him vp .xij. dayes,
and allowe him no meate at all, shuld be wonderd at
of all men. And euery man wold say that he had
done the laboring oxe wrong, and contrary to nature
also, and that, fynally, he had broken the command-

[1] A this, *for* his

ment of God. And shal not he than do a Christen preacher wrong, and breake Gods commandment, that moselyth hym for the space of whole¹ .xij. monthes, though he neuer so diligently treade out the corne of Gods ˙word, that the peple may eate and digest it? Yes, surely, though .x. M. general councels, and as many parlamentes, had determyned the contrary! Let not men byld their conscyences so moch vpon the actes of the parlament. For whan God shal say at the day of iudgement, "why hast thou taken away my ministers liuings from them the first yeare that thei fed my flock?" Thinck ye, that God wil allow this excuse, "I dyd it by the grant of the parlament," whan as that act of parlament is cleane contrary to Gods word? Nay, verely, he will not allow it; for eyther the minister is abyl and doth his duty (and so is worthy his meate the first yeare) or els he is vnable, and so neyther worthi to haue wages the first, nor yet the second or third. It were therfor well done, that it were inacted, that he that preached not shuld haue no wages, acording to the word of God: "qui non laborat, non manducet: he that laboryth not, let him not eate;" & that the first, second, thyrd, and all other frutes of benifyces afterward,² shuld be geuen to the precher that ˙laboryth in the Lords vyneyard. And as touching the first frutes of yong lordes landes, euery man can se, what harme may come therof. The lord hath oft³ tymes whan he dyeth .iij. score seruantes. Now if his sonne want the first frutes of his landes, wherwith shal he fynd his fathers old seruantes? He must byd them shift for them selues, and so thei must take standings in Shoters Hill, in Newmarket Heath, and in Stangate Hole. And so this payng of their first frutes is the cause of great theft, robry,⁴ murder. For comonly the

¹ A whole, *added*. ² A after, *for* afterward
³ A often, *for* oft: B *as above*. ⁴ A and, *after* robry; B *as above*.

CH. XVII.] APPORTIONMENT OF CREDITORS' CLAIMS. 41

great theues and robbers are the masterles and cast- *their first year's income is very great.*
away courtyers, or pompos bisshops seruantes, that haue
no wages of their masters.

Of particular tachementes, &c.

The. xvij. chapter.

Another thing very nedefull to be loked vpon is this, that whan any marchant or other, by losse of goodes, by fortune of the see, euel seruantys, euyl detters, by fyre, or other'wyse, come to an after deale, and not able to pay his credyte at his due tyme, but by force of pouertye is constrayned to demand longar tyme,—than ye haue a parcyall lawe in making of tachmentys, first come, first seruyd; so one or .ij. shall be all payd, and the rest shal haue nothyng. And comonly euer the rych shal haue the foredeale therof by this tachement, to the gret da*m*mage and oppressyon of the pore. For lyghtly the rich haue the first knoulege of soch thinges. Wherfor, in that case it were a godly way to make it in Ingland, as it is in dyuerse contryes, whan any such chance falleth, that than the most in nomber of the credytors and most in somme, shal bynde the rest to doo and gyue lyke tyme as doo the most of the credytors. And if it be duly found that the man be so farre at after deale, that he be not able to pay his whole credite in reasonable tyme, that than the lawe may bynd them that euery ma*n* may haue pound an[d] pound alyke, as farre as his goodys will goo, leauyng him some whan[1] as the lawe shall thynck good. And this lawe ˙shal be both neyhborly and godly.

[* leaf 35]
When a merchant is not able to pay in due time,
"first come first served,"
is the rule.

In such cases the majority rule;

and all share alike.

[* leaf 35, back]

[1] A what, *for* whan

That the rulars of the erth owght to sytt in the gatys, &ce. The .xviij. chapter.

<small>Consider how long men have to wait before they can get near their rulers.</small>

Another thing mete for all rulers, euyn from the lowest vnto the hyghest, to consydre and redresse is this :—Alas! how long shal men wayte and geue attendance vpon rulers, before thei can come to the spech of them! And how many porters be there also, to stoppe men from commyng to their spech. Whan he is past one he shal be put back at the second; or if he passe the second, he shal be returnyd[1] at the thyrd, onlesse he be rych or haue great fryndys. Oh ye kyngs and rulars, for the loue of God that ye shuld[2] haue to him that both made us of nought, and, whan we were lost by our synnys, redemyd us with the blode of his[3] Sonne, study the Scripturys and there shal ye see, that iudgys & rulers,

<small>In Scripture we read Judges and Kings always sat in the gates.
[* leaf 36]</small>

yea, euyn the kyngs, sate in iudgement in the open gatys, as apperyth in the second of the kyngs the .xix. chapter, Deuteronomy the .xvi. the second of Esdras the thyrd chapter. And why sate thei in the gatys, but that the peple, yea, euyn the porest, might come and open vnto the kyng his own cause? Than were there not so many rych lawyers, which be the poyson of the lawe. For the reuerence of God, ye kynges and rulers, eyther sytte in the opyn gatys agayne, or else

<small>Kings should let their doors be open at all times to all men.</small>

let your gatys, yea, euyn all your dorys, euyn to your pryuy chamber, be wyde open, for certen howrys, and that euery day in the yeare, euyn on Ester Day and all other dayes, if nede requyre, as thow mayst perceyue, Exodi the .xviij. "Iudge the peple at all seasons," &ce. And consyder what qualytes a iudge or a ruler shuld

<small>Judges should fear God,</small>

haue: thei must be men that feare God, and that are

---

[1] A tourned, *for* returnyd [2] A shoulde and oughte to, *for* shuld
[3] A the, *for* his

CH. XVIII.]   JUSTICE FOR THE POOR IN GERMANY.   43

true, and hate couetosnesse, as is descrybed in the same *and take no rewards.*
.x[v]iij. chapter. How many such rulers be in England? Yea, thei shuld also iudge the peple rightuosly.
Thei shuld not wrest the lawe, nor knowe any parson,[1]
nor yet take any[2] reward ; "for gyftys blynd the wyse,
and peruert the wordys of the rightuous," as ˙it foloweth   [* leaf 36, back]
in the text. Heare ye may se that it is nedeful (as I
haue touchyd before) that iudges and all other pleaters
in courtys, haue stypendys of the kyng, and there vpon *They should receive a stipend.*
to lyue. For here ye se that the Scripture sayth :—
"gyftes peruert the wordys of the ryghtuos ;" that is
to say, for the gyftys sake thei wil not se the right of
the pore ; and so thei turne right in to wrong, wherby
the pore be often oppressyd. In dyuers cyteys[3] of
Germany (as namely in Argentyne) the iudgys and
lordes syt opynly euery day in the yeare in their towne *In Germany the judges sit*
howse, saue only on the Sunday, and than also if nede *every day,*
requyre. And there thei eate co*n*tynually their dynars *even on Sundays,*
and suppars, so long as thei be in offyce, bycause thei
may alway be present to heare the complaynt of the
poore: yea euyn the porest man in the cytye or contry
may boldly come into their hall or stoue, thei being at *to hear the complaints of*
dynar, & no man so hardy as to take them by the *the poor.*
sleue, to lette them from the presence of the rulars.
And there may he open his matter hymself withowt
his chargeable man of lawe. ˙And he shal be haard,   [* leaf 37]
and shal not be answeryd, "Tary, syr knaue, tyl my
lordys haue dyned!" O noble Germanys, God hath
made yow a lyght vnto all rulers in the world, to rule
after the Gospell.

[1] A be parcionall, *for* nor—parson   [2] A any, *added.*
[3] A dyuers cyteys ȯf, *added.*

A godly admonycyon for the abolysshment of dyuerse abusys, that Gods glory only may be sowght. The .xix. Chapter.

No Councîl which has wicked privileges can seek a godly reformation.

How can that councel seke a[1] godly reformacyon of things misused, whan the councel itself hath wickyd pryuylegys? Wherfore acording to Christes commandment (Mathew the .vij.) " plucke owt the beame of your owne eyes first, & than ye shal the playnlyer se the mote in your neyhbors eyes." Se that ye breake first soch vnneyhborly, vnbrotherly, yea, and vngodly priuylegys, as ye yourseluys do enioy agaynst right and conscience, & than shal ye the better se to seke the common welth.

One privilege which is wicked, [* leaf 37, back]

Ye haue a preuylege which is this:—That if a lord, a knyght, or a burgesse of the parla'ment howse, or any of their seruantys, owe vnto any of the kings subiectys any somme of mony (be the detter neuer so rich, and

is the privilege of Parliament.

the credytor neuer so poore) he shal, by the preuylege of the parlament, not pay one peny so long as the parlament enduryth, be it neuer so long. Or if any of them or their seruantys haue done to any man any trespas or iniury, he may not also troble them. What

This is only a maintaining of wickedness.

is this but a mayntenance of wyckednesse? And how can wickydnesse abolyssh wyckednesse, but rather increase it? For the lordys sake loke vpon these thynges, and folow the councel of .S. Austen:—" Let custome gyue place to the truth, so that the truth may rule all things." Also ther is another thing worthy to be loked vpon, which is this:—Many noble men &

Another evil is retaining servants without paying them.

gentylmen retayne seruantys, & neuer gyue them peny wages, and scant a cote; for some be fayne to pay for their owne cotys, and spend all that thei haue of their owne[2] and of other mennys also, hopyng vpon some reward: and whan he seyth that all is spent, than

---

[1] A a, *added*.   [2] A cotys—owne, *added*.

CH. XIX.] RELIGION MUST BE REFORMED. 45

he wold depart and dare not. And gay he must goo [*leaf 38]
lyke his felows; and now his fryndes fayle hym, what
remedy? Forsoth shortly euyn to wat[c]h for a bowget.
Another sort there is, and thei be lyght ryding men *There is a sort*
all ready; and thei wil lyue lyke gentylmen. And for *of men who will become the*
his buclar or shyld, he wil seke to be retayning to some *retainer of some noble man or*
nobleman or gentylman that bearyth rule in the court *other.*
or contry, though he pay for his own lyuery. And the
noblemen and gentylmen, which shuld be the ponys- *The gentlemen*
shers of theft, be the chefe maynteyners of robry; bi *who should punish theft,*
this meanys often thei robbe & be not taken; but in *are the main- tainers of*
case he be taken, eyther he shal haue fauor for his *robbery.*
masters sake, or els bragg it owt with a carde of .x;
ye euyn face it owt, that neyther the playntyue nor
the xij men dare cast a thefe. Or if all this wyll not
helpe, than procure thei the kinges pardon. Oh noble
rulars, ye that be Christen in dede, take hede, that ye *Take heed that*
abuse not your auctoryte receyuyd of God! For if ye *you abuse not your authority.*
hang one that hath offendyd the lawe, and pardon
another, be ye not than parcyall? And no dowt if ye *If you pardon a*
pardon a thefe or a morderer, and thei commyt that *murderer, and [*leaf 38, back]*
offence agayn, so ye be partakers of their wickydnesse. *he commit the crime again, you*
For why? If ye had done iustyce afore, that offence *are partakers of his wickedness.*
had not bene commytted. Well, make a prouyso, that
no noble nor vnnoble man shall retayne any of the
kyngs subiectys withowt lauful wagys; and sett a
penalty ther vpon.

Moreouer, in as moch as it is open vnto all the
world that we haue long walked in a false religyon,
and haue had confydence in vayne thynges (as in the
tradycyons of mens imagynacyons) seke to reforme *Seek to reform*
these thynges and to set forth Christys religyon; that *matters of Religion.*
we may honor one God only, as the Scripture teacheth
us. And to leaue worshipping and calling vpon any
creaturys in heauyn or in erth, for he is a geluos God,
& wil haue no other in his sight, Exodi .xx. Se ther-

See that the people are taught to believe in one Mediator only.

[leaf 39]*

Away with your idols and images!

Idols must be abolished, if you will take away the occasion of spiritual fornication.

[leaf 39, back] Let the priests marry if they will.*

Peter and Paul were married.

Those who forbid marriage are devils.

for that the peple may be taught that[1] thei haue but one Medyator, lyke as thei haue but one God & one Redemer. And away with yowr superfluos holy dayes, for in one holy day is more idlenesse, whordome, and glotony vsed than in .x. workyng dayes! ˙Also away with all your idolls and imagys, both gret and small! For if no whore ought to be suffryd in the congregacyon of God (as it is wryten in Deuterono. the .xxiij.) than ought not the great whorys to be banysshed only, but the small also. Wherfore seing the Scripture callyth imagys whorys, Ieremy the .iij., and that ye haue rightfully put downe the gret imagys, with whom the peple haue commytted sprytual fornycacyon, all the rest, euyn the least also, are vtterly to be abolysshed, if ye will take away the occasyon of spryuall fornycatyon or idolatry from the people. How can ye, for shame, suffer your seluys & the peple to crepe to a crosse which will rott, seyng the Scripture for byddeth, sayng :—" non adorabis ea neque coles : " that is to say, " thow shalt gyue them neyther inward nor owtward worshipping." Is not this an owtward worshypping of an idol, to crepe to the crosse and to kysse it? What is it else? Furthermore, banyssh whordom and other abhomynable vyces, not to be namyd, from your prystes ; and let them that ˙will, haue their wyues, as thei had in the prymatyue church ; as had .S. Peter, as appearyth Mathew the .viij., and .S. Paul, Philipp. the iiij.[2] For to forbyd it as our bysshops doo, S. Paul calleth it the deuyls doctryne ; the first to Tymot. the .iiij. chapter. Now therfore, if ye wil byleue the Holy Goost, speaking in Paul, as ye be bownd to doo, if ye wyl byleue in God, than shal ye playnly se that the bisshops which forbyd that, and such other lyke, contrary to the Scrypture, be deuyls. Thyrdly condemne that auryculare confessyon, which is the preuy chamber

---

[1] A the peple—that, *added*.   [2] 1 Cor. ix. 5.

of treason of the bisshops, and let the peple be taught to confesse them seluys to the Lord with a repenta*n*t hart, who only forgeuyth syn: and to confesse and reconcyle them seluys to their neyhbors, who*m* thei haue offended, which haue the key of losyng in that case. But as it is now vsed (namely in axing of vayne questyons) it doth not mynyssh synne, but increaseth it. Prouyde also, that prayer & fastyng may be set forth, acording to the Scripture. And that the sacramen'tys may be mynistred in the mother tung. And that all the seruyce in the church may be taken owt of the Scripture, the Old Testament and the Newe, all inuented seruyce set a-parte. And let it be sayd and song all in the mother tong, that all may laude and prayse ¹God together; and so shal we knowe how to prayse¹ the Lord. Iff ye doo this, as ye be bownd, tha*n* vndowtydly shal the good workys appoynted in the Scripture florissh among the peple; as, namely, to beleue in one God only, to help the sayntys in this world, to decke and fede the image of God. These, and such other, shal we tha*n* doo of loue, and not seke nor thynk to be iustifyed by them. But now thorow Gods help, to bryng these godly actes and such other to a good and godly purpose, ye must fyrst downe with all your vayne chantrys, all your prowd colledgys of canons, and specyally your forkyd wolffys the bysshopes; leaue them no te*m*poral possessyons,² but only a competent lyuyng. An hundreth pownd for a bysshop, his wife, and chyldern, is inowgh. If he be an 'honest man, and preach Christ sincerely, he can not lacke besyde; if he do not, it is to moch. And let there be no more degreys among the*m*, but prystes and bysshops, as it was in the prymatyue church. Now for the goodys of these chantrys, collegys, and bisshops, for the Lordes sake take no example at the distrybucyon of the abbay

Condemn auricular confession.

Provide that prayer and fasting may be set forth.
[* leaf 40]

If you do this, good works will flourish among the people.

You must down with all chantries, all colleges, and all bishops.

[* leaf 40, back]

And let there be only two degrees, priests and bishops.

¹—¹ A God—prayse, *added*. ² A passions, *for* possessyons

Do as the Germans did:

put church property to the use of the commonwealth.

goodys and landys; but loke rather for your erudycyon to the godly and polytycke order of the Christen Germanys in this case. Which dyuyded not such goodys and landys among the pryncys, lordes, and rych men, that had no neede theroff; but thei put it to the vse of the comon welth, and vnto the[2] prouysyon for the pore, acordyng to the doctryne of the Scrypture.

That one pryst ought to haue but one benyfyce and one fermer, one ferme.
The .xx. Chapter.

A priest ought to have but one [* leaf 41] benefice.

THis thyng is also to be loked vpon, that euyn as one man may haue but one wife, so let a pryst haue but one benefyce; for if he 'haue more flockys than one to kepe, he wil neuer feede them both well. And if that be not a lyuyng for a man, his wife, and his chylderne, as some be not, than ioyne hym to the next paryssh, wherby the poore may be at lesse charge with the pryst. The popissh prestys will make a mocke at this, which hipocrytes I send to the .x. chapter of Mathew, where Chryst sayth to his Apostyls

Ministers should not possess gold and silver.

and mynysters of his congregacyon, that thei shal not possesse gold, syluer, nor brasse, &c. : how moch lesse then shuld thei enioy their inordynate possessyons! And euyn as a pryst shuld haue but one benefyce, so make that one man, of what degree so euer he be,

A farmer should have only one farm, say of £20 a year.

shal hold and kepe in his own handys or occupyeng no more than one ferme, maner, or lordshyp, beyng a competent lyuyng, as of .xx. pownd yerely rent. So that it may be lauful for one man to kepe .ij., if thei both together be not aboue .xx. pownd; but no man to kepe aboue[3] .iij., be thei neuer so smal rent. This were

By the extortions of farmers,

a brotherly and godly act. For by your oppressors and

---

[1] A Christen, *added.*   [2] A the, *added;* B *as above.*
[3] A aboue, *added.*

extorcyoners, how be the townys and villagys decayed? *[* leaf 41, back]* towns and villages are decayed. Where as were .viij., x., xij., yea, xvi. howsoldys and more, is now but a shepe howse and .ij. or iij. shepardys. And one man shal haue .ij. or iij. such thyngs, or more, in his ha*n*dys, that a pore man¹ scarcely haue an hole to put in hys head for these gret extorcyonars. So if ye seke this godly redresse, where as ye haue a fewe in a contry, which be inordynate rych extorcyonars, and a great multytude of poore peple, than shal ye haue but a fewe poore and a gret nowmber of a meane and reasonable substance, and fewe poore, & lesse extorcyonars; which wold be no smal ease to the common welth. Here shal all inclosars, grossers vp of fermys, extorcyonars, and oppressers of the common welth, be offendyd at me and call me heretycke and traytor. But all such I send vnto the fyft chapter of the prophete Esay, where he sayth:—"Wo be vnto yow which ioyne one howse to another, and bryng one land so nye vnto another, tyl ye can get no more grownd; wil ye dwell vpo*n* the erth alone," &c? Ye extorcyonars! lerne to feare God, and marke what, and how vehemently the Holy Gost speakyth here in the prophete, "wil ye dwell vpon the erth alone?" Here is a fearful sentence for yow!

Instead of a few rich and many poor, we might have few poor, and many living in comfort.

"Woe to you who join house to house and field to field!"

[* leaf 42]

Of the inhansyng of the custome, which is agaynst the common welth, &c.

The .xxi. chapter.

ANother greuous burden, spro*n*g vp of fewe yerys past, is the inhansyng of the custome of warys inward, which was granted for certen yearys to helpe the kyng toward his warrys; and yet but vpon a condycyon, that the kyng shuld be a shyld and defense of the marchantys goodys

The Customs are a grievous burden.

¹ A man can, *for* man

agaynst all pyrates and robbers vpon the see, and to make them good such goodys as shuld be taken. And now it is not holden for certen yerys, but as it were for euer, and from a subsydye, to a custome. And yet the merchantys not defendyd acordyng to the comnant neyther, wherby many an honest marchant hath bene vndone. This burde*n* is not ˙preiudycyal to the marchantys only, but it is to the great da*m*mage of the whole reame also. For why ? All warys be raysed therby .v. in euery hundreth, and somme moch more ; so that the comons bye all things so moch the derer. I thynke if the kynges grace knewe what a burden it is to the comons, & with what euyl wyll his marchantys pay it, he wold, I dowt not, be content with the old subsydy, that is to say, a certen of euery fardel, chest, mawnd, bale, or what so euer it be, as was in old tyme ; and as it is in Flandres, and ouer all the Emperors landys at this daye. Oh that men, which be abowt a kyng, wold be as ready to gyue councel to do rightuosnesse, & to seke discharge of their pryncys conscyence, and the welth of his sowle, as thei be to enuegle hym to yocke his comons, sekyng the only profyght of the body ; as though there were no world after this, or as though the King of all kynges sawe no furder than a mortal prynce !

A godly aduysement how to bestowe the goodys and landys of the bisshops, &ce.

The .xxij. Chapter.

Although there be many godly mynded, I trust, in the Parlament howse, which can dyuyse wayes ynowe to employe the goodys and landys of bysshopes, deanys, canons, and chantreys, to Gods glory, to the common welth, & to the help of the pore (as there are wayes ful many, whoso lysteth to study the*m*); yet I thynk my selfe bound partly to wryte myne aduyse in some things which be most nedeful. First, part of them may be distributed to the poore, as well to poore¹ maydens mariages and poore house holders, as to the blynd, sick, and lame; onlesse it be the one halfe of² the plate² to come to the kings grace, for this purpose, that it be turned into the coyne of the reame. And of their temporals, let .viij. or .x. pound and not aboue of euery hundreth be granted to the kyng, that he therof may haue ˙homage, as chefe lord and king, as reason is. And to ease the comons of subsidys, whan nede shal be, that the pore & myddel sort of the peple may be easyd therby, the rest to be employed vpon poore cyties and townys, and to the prouysyon of the poore; as, part of it to be le*n*t to³ poore occupyers, to euery citie acording to the nomber of the occupyers in the same. And let euery occupyer haue acording to his nede; and euery one to be bound brotherly for another ioyntly to the kyng. That is to say, the whole town, as many as haue any part of the mony; and the first yere to pay no entres, but euery yeare after .iij. pound of euery hundreth pound, that the somme may encreace and not decay. And make a prouyso, that no cloth be made but in cyteys and great townys, and the town seale to be vpon euery cloth, which town shal make good all such fawtys as shal be fownd in their clothys. And agayne also, that the clothyers shal kepe no fermys in the contry, except it be one for his own prouysyon. And thus shal ye haue true cloth made, and ˙euery neyhbor lyue by other. The lordys and gentylmen by

lands and goods of bishops.

Part may be given to the poor;

half the plate might go to the King.

[* leaf 43, back]

The rest to be used upon the poor of cities and towns,

who shall pay three per cent. for the use of the money.

Cloth to be made only in cities and towns.

[* leaf 44]

---

¹ A as well to poore, *added.*
² A to, place, *for* of, plate; B *as above.*
³ A to the, *for* to; B *as above.*

their londys; the marchant only by his marchandyse; the clothyer by making his cloth; the fermer by tylling his land and bredyng, &cete.

Part of the goods may be used to

Item, part of these forsayd goodys may be employed to this vse, that in euery hundreth, good towne, or cyty, certen howsys be maynteynyd to lodge and kepe poore men in, such as be not able to labor, syck, sore, blynd, and lame. And euery one of them to haue wherwith to lyue, and to have poore whole women to mynystre vnto them. And for Christes sake, ye rulers, loke vpon your hospytals, whether the poore haue their right there, or no. I heare that the masters of your hospytals be so fatt that the poore be kept leane and bare inough: the crye of the peple is heard vnto the Lord, though ye wyll not heare. Now to our former purpose agayne. Let phisicyans and surgens be found in euery such town or cyte, where such houses be, to loke vpon the pore in that towne and in all other ioyning vnto it; and 'thei to lyue vpon their stipend only, without taking any peny of there pore, vpon payne of losing both his earys and his stypend also.

keep houses to lodge and maintain the sick and poor in.

Let physicians and surgeons be provided in every town to look after the poor.

[* leaf 44, back]

Certain schools should be free.

Item, in dyuers head cyties and good townes, let scholes be mainteyned and lectures to be had in them of the .iij. tongys,—Hebrew, Greke & Latyne; and the readers to haue an honest stipend. Item, in euery such cyty and town to haue a certen nomber of pore mens chyldern found of free cost, tyl thei be of good age and wel lernyd. Item, the encrease of the mony, that is to say .iij. pownd of euery hundreth, to be bestowyd vpon poore copyls at their maryages to beginne the world withall. These wayes and such lyke, may thos goodys and landys be bestowed, of another sort than to fynd such a sort of belly goddys, and idle stout and strong lorels as ye haue done, yea, a sort of dronken bussardys. And thus haue the Germanys (where as the Gospel is receyued) bestowed the goodys

Money is better bestowed thus than in feeding monks.

and landys of soch abbeys as thei haue suppressyd. And I thinck no godly hart can be agaynst this dyuyse. Now therfore 'I exhort the higher powers, in the name of the euerlyuing God, that if thei wyl not loke vpon these[1] spyrytual extorcyonars (I meane[2] bysshops, canonys, and chanterers) for the zeale which thei ought to beare to the congregacyon of God, neyther for the loue that thei ought to haue to the common welth and to the poore ; yet let them remember it for their own welthys sake. And let the kyngs grace consyder how tyrannosly, by the vertu of their wicked mammon, thei vsed part of his progenytors, kynges of Ingland ; as Wyllm Rufus, Henry the second, and Kyng Iohan. Rede the storyes, and ye shal se part of their knauery ; yet is the best made to cloke their wickednesse. It were hard to say whether thei were the auctors of the commocyon in the north or no. I thynck it is as well possyble for the ocyane se to be without water, as it is for them to cease musyng of myschefe.

[* leaf 45]
Look upon these extortioners, the Bishops.

Let the king remember

how his progenitors were used.

Perhaps the bishops were the promoters of the Rising in the North.

A lamentacyon for that the body and tayle of the pope is not banisshed with his name.[3]

The .xxiij. Chapter.

OH mercyful Father of heauyn, I can never lament inough to heare the Gospel thus blasphemyd ; to be namyd a thyng causyng sedicyon, whan it is the only cause of concord and

[* leaf 45, back]

The gospel blasphemed and called a cause of sedition.

---

[1] A the, *for* these [2] A say, *for* meane
[3] This chapter was printed as a Broadside in the 17th century, with the heading, "The true Coppy of the Complaint of Roderyck Mors, some time a Gray Fryer, unto the Parliament House of England, about an hundred yeares agoe, when the Bishop of Rome being Banish'd out of the Realme, the Bishops of England acted his part by power of the old Romish Canon, newly translated into English Law." Following this is a short prologue, in which it is said that the book was "printed in Anno 1545." The sheet ends with these words,—" Printed

peace in conscyence vnto the faythful. Yet these bysshops, deanys, and canons of collegys, with other the popys shauelings, acording to their old wont, shame not to blaspheme this Holy Word by all the sotle meanys that can be dyuysed. How besy were thei to stey the puttyng forth of the Great Byble, and to haue had the Byble of Thomas Mathy[1] called in! But the Lord strengthnyd the hart of the prynce to set it forth agaynst their willys. Yet how shamefully haue thei and their membres, in many placys of England, dreuyn men from readyng the Byble! Yea & Boner, bysshop of London, shamyd not in the yere a thowsand fyue hundreth and forty, to preson one Porter and other for readyng in the Byble; which, if it be not heresy to God, than what is heresy? And if it be not treason to the kyng to deface 'his iniunccyons, than what is treason? And agayne, if it be not theft to the comon welth to steale from them their sprytual fode, than what is robry and theft? And euyn in the begynnyng of the last Parlament, in the yere a thousand fyue hundreth and .xli., how dyd thei blaspheme, rage, & belye the Holy Goost, saing it is not ryghtly translated, and that it is ful of heresys, and that thei wold correck it, and set out one ryghtly. Soner can thei fynd fawtys than amend it. Who perceyueth not your wycked intentys, that, in the meane tyme, ye loke for the death of the kyng, whom God preserue to his plesure! O ye blynd Phylistyans, the Scripture is ful of sentencys which teach men to knowe you, and to beware of you. I cannot blame you, though ye fyght thus[2] agaynst God and his Word, to shutt it vp from the peple. For why?

in time and place of publique observation of the English Prelats, so contrary handling the matter with the peace-seeking Protestant Subjects of Scotland and the blood-sucking Popish Rebells of Ireland." The copy of this Broadside in the British Museum (Press Mark 669 f. 4, leaf 41) has in a contemporary hand the date 15 Jan. 1641.

[1] A Mathew, *for* Mathy   [2] A thus, *added*

Who so euer readyth or hearyth the contentys of that boke, and byleueth the Holy Goost, shal playnly se that ye be the very enemyes of God ; and so shal cast you out of their conscyence, where ye haue long sytten in the place of God. Wherby also ye shuld lose your gret ryches and auctorite, which makyth you to roare lyke lyons, to teare lyke bearys, and to byte lyke cruel woluys, and to styng lyke adders. No dout one bisshop, one deane, one college or howse of canons, hath euer done more mischeffe agaynst Gods Word, and sought more the hynderance of the same, than .x. howsys of monkys, fryers, chanons, or nunnys euer dyd. The kyngs grace began wel to wede the garden of Ingland, but yet hath he left stonding (the more pytye !) the most fowlest and stynkyng wedys, which had most nede to be first pluckyd vp by the rootys ; that is to say, the prycking thistels and stingyng nettels ; which, styll stondyng, what helpyth the deposyng of the pety membres of the Pope, and to leaue his whole body behynd, which be the pompos bisshops, canons of collegys, deanys, and such other ? Surely it helpyth as moch as to say, I wyl go kyll all the foxes in .S. Iohans Wodde, because I would haue no more foxes bred in all England ! We say we haue cast the Pope out of Ingland : —how so, I aske ye ? seyng he came neuer in Ingland, how can he be cast out thereof [1] ? Some wil say yes, his tributys, and other pollagys, be taken from him. Wel, thankys be to God, we be somewhat eased of our temporal and bodyly burden. But there be gretter things in this matter than that ; which, wel [2] ponderyd, we may say, and lye not, that the Pope remayneth wholly styll in Ingland, saue only that his name is banished. For why ? his body (which be the bisshops and other shauelings) doth not only remayne, but also his tayle, which be his filthy tra-

[* leaf 46, back]

You bishops are the enemies of God.

Your riches make you war like lions, tear like bears, bite like wolves, sting like adders.

The King began to weed the garden well, but he left the thistles and nettles.

[* leaf 47]
We say we have cast out the Pope:—how ?

His name is banished, but his body and tail remain.

[1] A therefore, *for* thereof   [2] A was, *for* wel

dicyons, wicked lawys, and beggarly ceremonyes (as S. Paul called them) yea and the whole body of his pestiferos canon lawe, acording to the which iudgement is geuen thorow the reame, and men condemnyd to death after the prescrypt of it. So that we be styll in Egypt and remayne in captyuyte, most greuosly laden by obseruyng and walking in his most filthy drosse aforsayd, which is a mysty and endles maze. And so long as ye walke in those wicked la‘wys of Antichrist the Pope, and maynteyne his knyghtes the bisshops in soch inordynate riches and vnlauful auctoryte, so long say I, ye shal neuer banyssh that monstruos beast the Pope out of Ingland. Yea, and it shal be a meane, in processe of tyme, to bryng us into a temporal bondage also agayn, and to haue him reygne, as he hath done, lyke a God. And that know our forkyd cappys ryght well; which thing makyth them so boldly and shamelesly to fyght in their gods quarel, agaynst Christ and his Word. The bysshops of England neuer toke so gret paynes to defend the Pope and his kyngdome, as they haue done syns the kings grace toke rightfully from him his accustomyd pollagys, which vsurpedly he had out of this reame. To proue this to be true, what blood haue thei shed, syns that tyme, of the belouyd seruantes of the[1] euerlyuing God, for preching, teaching, writing, and walking in the truth: as Tewkysbery, Baynam, Fryth, Bylney, Barnys, Garet, Ierom, with diuerse other in Kent, Salysbery, and dyuerse other placys. ˙And Wyllm Tyndal, the apostle of Ingland (although he were burnt in Brabance) yet he felt the bisshops blessing of Ingland, which procured him that death which he loked for at their handes. Neuertheles, I dowt not, but that all these be of the number of them that S. Iohan spekyth of in the Apocalipse, which lye vnder the altar till the number of their brethern be

---

[1] A the, *added*.

fulfilled, which shal be slayne for the Gospels sake. *brethren be fulfilled.*
I reherse not their namys for anye prayse to be geuyn to them; but that the congregacyon of Christ may laude and prayse the euerliuyng God, for geuing them grace to stand so faythful in the Lord to the end, leauyng vs the victory, which is part of your spyrytual comfort. For God promyseth the preachers & mynysters of his word no other reward in this life. And *He promises His preachers nothing else in this life.* thorow the preaching of these poore wretchys (but outcastes in the sight of the world, as S. Paul sayth[1]) he hath wrought this, that where as the kyng was before but a shadow of a kyng,[2] or at the most but halfe a king, now he doth wholly raygne thorow 'their preaching, [* leaf 48, back] wryting, and suffryng. But now to the tyranny of the bysshops onys agayne; which, besydes the murderyng of these sayntes, how haue thei bewitched the Parlament *The bishops have bewitched the Parliament.* howse in making such vyperos actys as the beast of Rome neuer made him selfe! For the Pope neuer made the mariage of prystes to be[3] death, and such other. Thus by your sotiltes and most crafty wyles, ye make the peple *You make the people abhor the Pope for a face, and compel the people to walk in his laws.* to abhorre the name of the Pope[4] for a face, and compel them to walk in all his wicked lawys. And the word of God, which we say we haue receyuyd, is not, nor can not be sufferyd to be preached and taught purely and sincerely, without mixyng it with your inuented tradycyons and seruyce. For who so euer doth (stonding faythfully vnto it) he shal dye for it! Thus ye may se, that the thing which we say that we haue cast of, we receyue, cherissh, maynteyne, and walke therein. And agayn, that thing which we say we haue receyued, *That which we have received is abhorred, and called the "new learning."* by the craft and tyranny of the bysshops, is abhorred, despysed, taken for a sedycyos thing,[5] 'called newe lernyng; and men be dreuyn from it for feare of losse [* leaf 49]

---

[1] A as S. Paul sayth, *added.* [2] A of a kyng, *added.*
[3] A be, *added.* [4] A Pope of Rome, *for* Pope
[5] A sedicion, *for* sedycyos thing

of goodys, of ponysshment of body, and danger of death: so weake and frayle is our flessh. What a lamentable thing is this, that men shuld be dryuyn from the Gospel of Christ, the glad tydings that bringeth peace in conscyence to the faythful; that is forgeuenesse of synnes in Christes blode. By these frutys all men may knowe, that thei be more natural to their wicked father the Pope, than any child can be to his natural father. And that shal the reame fele at the change of a prynce, or at such tyme as thei loke for, onlesse God of his mere[1] mercy breake the wicked councels of them. What is the cause, that the bisshops be so dilygent to sytt so often vpon the .vi. wycked Artycles, but only that thei be a stablysshing of the Popys auctorite, be thow sure. Now therfore, that same God wich gaue grace to Achab to harken vnto the voyce of Elyah, the .iij. of the kings the .xviij., to the confounding of the false prophetys, gyue our noble king that same grace, if it be his godly wil and pleasure, to harken to the godly lernyd, to confound and destroy all the false prophetys in Ingland! And than I am sure there shal not be remaynyng one pompos bysshop in the reame. Wherfore, to open the conclusyon of this lytle lamentacyon, if ye wil banyssh for euer the Antychrist, the Pope, out of this reame, ye must fell down to the ground those rotten postys, the bisshops, which be cloudys without moyster; and vtterly abolyssh all and euery his vngodly lawys, decreys, tradycyons, and ceremonyes, withowt signifycacyons; for thei wayte but for a tyme to robbe some noble man of his witt, as thei wold haue done with the Marques of Exetor. This is as sure as Wynchester receyued a letter from the Pope at his being at Regenspurg. Well, these filthy dreggs onys abolisshed,[2] than make no lawys but such as shal be agreabyl to Gods Word. And so shal

[1] A very, *for* mere   [2] A expelled, *for* abolisshed

ye dryue out Antychryst and his membres, or els neuer; and thus we shal not only auoyde our temporal bondage, but also our sprytual captyuyte, which thing is most to be desyred. And surely seing there is no pour vpon erth aboue the temporal, to redresse cyuyle matters, comon welthys, and to cha*n*ge wycked lawys and euyl customys, and in as moch as the hygher pours be fully certifyed by the Scripture, that as the Pope is enemy to the Gospel, so be his chyldern the bisshops (which thing is open and manyfest, to as many as wil not wilfully be blynd); therfore, I say, I cannot se how thei can suffer them thus to raygne, persecutyng the setters forth of the Gospel, but that thei be partakers of their iniquyte, and sprynckled with them in the blode of the rightuos. [* leaf 50] There is no power on earth above the temporal. How then are bishops allowed to reign?

A comparyson betwene the doctryne of the Scripture and of the bysshops of England.

The .xxiiij. chapter.

NOw wil I speake no further against the partycular pope, forasmoch as euery bysshop is now a pope. And that ye may the playnlyer se, that the proud prelatys, the bisshops,[1] be very Antichrystes, as is their father of Rome, I wyl recyte certe*n* doctrynes of the Scrypture, manifestly taught by the Holy Goost, the prophetys, apostyls, and by Chryst Iesus hymselfe. And compare them with the doctrines of the bysshops, and thou shalt manyfestly se, that their doctryne is as directly agaynst the Holy Goost, as is lyght agaynst darcknes. First the Scripture teacheth one God only thorout the Byble, and the apostels refused to be worshypped, as the .xiiij. chapter of the Actes of the Apostels doth manifestly declare, where Pawl and Barnabas rent their clothys, cryeng vnto the peple, That you may see the bishops are Antichrists, [* leaf 50, back] I will recite certain texts of Scripture. The Bible teaches that there is but one God.

---

[1] A I meane, *after* bisshops

"Why do ye thys? We be mortal men lyke vnto yow; turne from these vanytes vnto the liuyng God, &c." Lyke wyse the angel refused to be worshipped of man, Apocalypse the .xxij., with dyuerse other testymonyes, as the .xx. of Exody, the Psal. lxvi.,[1] and .lxxxvi.[1] And agayne, imagys are forbydden thorow the Scripture, & hated of God, which commandeth us that we shuld not ones bowe vnto them, Exodi. the .iiij.[2] and .xx., Leuiticus .xxvi. And Salomon curseth both the image and the maker theroff, sayng the sekyng of them to be the begynnyng of whoredome, in the .xiiij. chapter of the Booke of Wysdom. Further more reade the .xliiij. chapter of Esay, and I dowt not but, if thou beleuyst in God, thow wylt not worship nor knele afore an image for all the goodys in the world. But now contrary to thys doctryne, our forkyd Chananytes, the pompos bisshops, teach us to worship many goddys. If any man aske me how I proue that, I answer:— what a multytude of Holy Dayes haue thei made vnto sayntes, as to the Virgyn Mary, Pawl, Peter, Iamys, Iohan, Corpus Christi, &cet.! For what purpose do thei hold those Holy Dayes, but only to honore them as goddes? Do thei not make men to fast their euyns as though thei were goddes? Do thei not teach us to pray to them,[3] and to crye to them for helpe? Come to the labor of a woman that is a Pharysy, and thow shalt heare hir crye & call for help, more vpon the Virgyn Mary than she[4] will vpon the euerlyuyng God, who is the only Creator and Sauyor of the Vir'gyn: yea and that most blasphemosly, sayng, "Our Lady, haue mercy vpon me!" And lyke wyse vpon other of[5] Goddys creaturys. Now in these dayes thei wil say, haply, we teach not to worship them as goddes, but as

---

[1] See Psalm lxxxi. 9, 10. [2] Deut. iv. and Exod xx.
[3] A to them, *added*. [4] *Orig.* shal
[5] A of, *added*. B *as above*.

mediators. I tel the, that is also a false and a deuelyssh doctryne. For the Scripture sayth, there is but one mediator[1] betwene God and man, Iesus Chryst; the .i. to Tymothy the .ij. chap.; Hebruys the .iiij; the .ij[2] of Iohan. the .ij. chap.; the Ephesyans the .iij.[3] S. Paul dyd wel to name Christ, that we may know who it is, though the bysshops wil not for their offerings sake; and therfore thei wold haue many mediators. It is euydent also that thei teach men to worship imagys, for euery church is ful, and specyally S. Mary Ouerys in Sothwarke for gylded imagys. And although by the vertu of the kyngs iniunccyons, dynerse idollys be taken away, yet Bonar, Bisshop of London, by the cowncel of Cole his trayteros popyssh chanceler, one of Poolys ryght scolars, although he came from hym vnder a pretence to be his depute as his frutys de'clare, if thei indifferently were loked vpon, by his deuelyssh councel; I say hys master shamed not, contrary to the same iniunccyons, to set vp other in their placys; as in the body of Powlys Church, where as stode an idol of the Virgyn Mary, of his feruent charyte toward the mayntenance of Idolatry, that it shuld not vtterly decay; and of hys cold loue and fauor toward the kyngys iniunccyons, set vp in the same place another idol of S. Iohan Baptyst. And Wynchester, at his beyng a[t] Ratyspone, caused an image to be gyldyd, and payd for the gylding of an idol named the Schone Mary, that men of all nacyons being there, might se what fauor he bare toward hys Pryncys iniunccyons. Do thei not by these, and such[4] actys, condemne the kyngs deposyng of idols as moch as in them lyeth? Oh pryuy traytors, and open idolators, ye wyl say, thei be bokys for the vnlerned and therfor necessary. But how can that be necessary, whych the Holy Gost so

It is a devilish doctrine; for there is but one Mediator.

Every church is full of images, especially St Mary Overies in Southwark.

[* leaf 52]

Bonar set up in St Paul's an image of John the Baptist in the place of one of the Virgin.

The Bishop of Winchester had an image gilt, and paid for the gilding.

---

[1] A and intercessour, *after* mediator [2] John ii. 1, 2.
[3] Ephe. ii. 13. [4] A and such, *added*.

diligently forbyddeth, vtterly as before is sayd?[1] Answere me Cole, wyth thy[2] popyssh canon 'lawe! Agayne, God in the old lawe appoynted the seuynth day to be kept holy, called the Sabbate day, for the which we hold the Sunday; whych our forefathers ordeyned in the steade of the[3] Satterday, that the peple shuld come together[4] to the tempyl, to heare Goddys Word preached in their mother tong, wherby thei were edifyed to walke in the amendment of lyfe, and to bryng forth the frutys of our fayth, that is, good workys, appoynted in the scrypture only to Goddys honor and the profyght of our neyhbore; but yet not to kepe it so idylly, that after we haue heard Gods word, but that we myght doo any nedeful busynesse vpon the Sunday, as wel as other dayes. And as for our Holy Dayes of our own inuenting, in which we worship the creaturys of God, the Lord hatyth them, as apperyth playnly in the first of Esay. Yea God hatyth and[5] abhoryth them, sayth the prophete Amos in the v. chap. And Paul rebuketh them that kepe soch holy dayes, Galathyans the .iiij, sayng, "Ye obserue dayes, &c., I am afrayd, lest I haue be'stowed labor vpon yow in vayne." But our Idle bisshops, contrary to the Scripturys before cyted,[6] haue brought us in bondage, that in maner the forth day in the yere thei haue made holy day, and not to God only, as all men knowe, but to his creaturys. And how do the peple hallowe them? In commyng to church to a sort of domme ceremonyes, & to here moch inuented seruyce, in a strange tong which they vnderstond not, nor yet x. among an hundreth of them seluys. And thus the peple depart the church as empty of all sprytual knowlege as thei came thether. And the rest of the day

---

[1] A vtterly—sayd, *added*.   [2] A the, *for* thy
[3] A the, *added*.   [4] A together, *added*.
[5] A hatyth and, *added*.   [6] A recited, *for* cyted

Side notes:
- [* leaf 52, back]
- God appointed the seventh day as the Sabbath,
- instead of which our fathers ordained the Sunday.
- They were not to keep it idly, but after hearing the Bible might do any profitable business.
- Paul rebukes those who keep holy days.
- [* leaf 53]
- How do our bishops hallow them?
- The church is left destitute of all spiritual food.

thei spend in all wanton and vnlawful gamys, as dyse, cardys, dalyeng with wemen, dansing, and such lyke. But if any man do any bodyly worke, though very nede for the mayntenance of his lyuyng co*m*pel hym there vnto, he shal be punysshed, and called heretycke to. But[1] not withstondyng this, thei are co*n*tent with (thankys be to God!) that if such an heretyck worke euery Sunday in the yeare, though it be on Easter Day, for the kyngs grace, or by his com'missyon, it is no offence but lauful; as though it were lauful for the kyng to breake Gods co*m*mandment! But for all that, if thei fearyd not more the kyng than thei doo God, thei wold ponyssh them also. Oh most suttyl and wyly theuys! what kyng or emperor, yee, what bisshop or Apostle, can dyspense with Godds Word, which he eyther biddeth or forbiddeth? Where as Chryst saieth, "Thow shalt not put away thy wyfe, but only for adultery," can all the whole world, ye[2] Antychrystes, dispense with me to put away my wyfe, but for that cause only? If ye beleuyd ryghtly in God, and lyued in his feare, ye shuld dispense therwith for no nother cause. More ouer the Scripture teacheth us "mariage to be institute of God," Genesis the .ij., and honoryd of Chryst with his presence and first myracle, turnyng water into wyne, Iohan the .ij. And .S. Pawl sayth: "Let euery man haue his wife, to auoyde fornycacyon," i. to the Coryn. the .vij.; marke, he sayth euery man; here is no man except. For it is honorable, sayth Paul to the Hebruys, and 'the bedd thereof vndefyled. And in the primatyue church it apperyth that the Apostels had wiues, as Peter and Paul as is[3] before rehersed. And Paul calleth it a deuclyssh doctryne to forbyd mariage to them that haue not the gyft of chastyte. And yet, notwit[h]stonding, our lecheros bisshops, or rather sodomytes, as chast as a sawt bytch, take it for a vyle

Sunday is spent in wanton games, dice, cards, dancing, and so on.

[*leaf 53, back]

As if it were lawful for the King to break God's command.

Christ forbad divorce, except for adultery.

The Scriptures say marriage was instituted by God.

St Paul advises all men to marry,

[*leaf 54]

and it appears the Apostles had wives.

And yet the bishops take it

---

[1] A And, *for* But   [2] A O ye, *for* ye   [3] A is, *added.*

& an vnholy thyng! For thei forbyd them seluys, and all that beare the marke of the beast Antichrist, to mary, and haue procured death to them that seke rather to mary than to burne; but to kepe whorys their own lawe permytteth! Steuyn Gardner, which was the chefe causer of that wicked act, is it not manifest & openly known that he kepyth other mennys wyues, which I could name, and wil doo hereafter, if he leaue not his shameles whordom. If all the bysshops of Ingland were hanged which kepe harlots and whorys, we shuld haue fewer pompos bysshops than we haue. Well, yow bysshops, which had your maryd wyues at the making of that wicked act, and put them away for feare, loke well vpon it; for ye had bene better to haue suffred death, than so cowardly to denye the lawe of the Lord. Wherfore I aduyse yow, in the name of the Lord, bytterly to repent with Peter, takyng better hold and receyuing your owne maryed[1] wyuys agayne; yea though ye shuld giue ouer and forsake all your pompos auctoryte and vayne ryches. And stand fast to Gods word, euen in the face of princys, as did the Apostles, the Christen bisshop, S. Ambrose, with all the faythful sort from the begynnyng. Remember what Christ sayth: "He that denyeth me before men, him shal I denye agayn before my heuynly father." And agayne:— "He that holdeth the plough, and lokyth back, is not mete for me," & such other. For if ye stop your mowthes, your talent shal be taken from yow, and geuen to him that hath x.

Agayne, the Scripture teacheth us to confesse our synnes only vnto God with a repentant hart, and to loke for absolucyon of them thorow Christ, Daniel the .ix. Dauyd confes'syd hym to the lord, Psalm xxxij. and li. Manasses made a ryght confessyon, as apperyth in his prayer. If we so confesse ourselues, we shal

---

[1] A own maryed, *added*.

gladly¹ forgeue euyn our enemyes. And in thus confessing our synnes to the Lord with a contryte hart, repentyng and turning from our synnes, all that we haue done before shal no more be thought vpon, but seperat from us so farre as is the east from the west, as sayth the prophet. And whan we offend our neyhbers and brethern, we may not only confesse vs vnto the Lord, but also vnto them whom we haue offended, and be reconciled one to another, as Christ teacheth vs in the .v. of Mathew, and Iames also in the .v. chapter of his Epistle. This confessyon taught us the Holy Gost long before Antychryst had fownd out that fylthy auricular confessyon to his gresy shauelings, which was not from the beginnyng, neyther shal be to the end. Thei teach men to poure their synnes in to the earys of their generacyon, that thei may sytt in the conscyence of men, wher as God alone shuld sytt. And agayne, 'thei heare gladly the confessyon of harlottes, that thei may knowe where to spede. And the synnes being pouryd² in to their eares by mouth, not regardyng the repentance of the hart, yet thei take vpon them to forgeue such synnys; where as it is the offyce of God only to forgyue synne. And thei do both robbe God of his offyce, and also disceyue the pore blind peple, which thynck themseluys to be healed, whan thei remayne lepers styll. For their malyce remaynyth styll, euyn agaynst their fryndes many tymes, and that for small matters, not withstonding their confessyon. As for the key of byndyng and losyng, the grettest part of them knowe no more what it meanyth than a bussard. Oh ye blasphemers! what grownd haue ye to stablyssh your auryculer confessyon? Haply ye wyl alledge that place where as Chryst sent the lepers vnto the pryst, Luke the .xvij; which maketh as moch for that purpose, as to lay an

When we offend our neighbours we must confess unto them, as well as unto God.

Auricular confession.

[*leaf 55, back] *Antichrist's shauelings gladly hear the confessions of harlots.*

It is God's office to forgive sin.

As for the key of binding and loosing, they know not its meaning.

Christ sent the lepers to the priest

¹ A godly, *for* gladly   ² A put, *for* pouryd
BRINKLOW.   5

vnyon to my lytel fyngar for the tothe ache. For Christ sent them to the prystes, only to offer 'an oblacyon after the lawe, and that the prystes myght se that thei were whole; and so after certen dayes to be kept in for a tryal, which exspyred, and than thei being fownd whole, the prystes myght admytte them to come into the company of the whole peple agayne. Rede the xiij. and .xiiij. of Leuiticus, and thow shalt perceyue the same. Christ healyd the peple of dyuerse other diseasys, as of the palsy, blody flyxe, possessed with deuyls, and such other; yet he neuer sent none to the prystes, but the lepers only: which he dyd, bycause it was so appoynted of God in Moises lawe.

Item. Chryst teacheth us how we shuld pray, not with moch bablyng, as the hethyn doo, thinkyng to be heard for their moch bablyng sake, Mathew. the .vi. (yet ought the prayer of a Christyane to be contynuall, as he shewyth by an example of the lendyng of .iij. loauys, Luke the .xi.,[1] & agayne by the parable of the iudge, Luke the .xviij.); but we must pray in lyfting vp our mindes vnto God,[2] 'and we must regard that our mouth, spyryt, and hart be eleuated to gether myndfully in fayth; for "God is a spyryte, and wyl be worshypped in spyryt and truth," Iohan the .iiij. This teacheth the[3] Scripture. But our forked hypocrytes teach us to nomber our prayers, to say so many Ladys Psalters, with long mattens & euynsonges; and that all in Latyne, which the lay peple vnderstond not. How can we pray or worship God aryght, whan our hartes knowe not whether[4] our mouth laudyth[5] God for his benefightes allready receyued, or els that we demawnd[5] any peticyon? Agaynst soch kynd of prayng

---

[1] A as Luke declareth very playnly in the aleauenth chapter, *for* Luke the xi.   [2] A oure Lorde, *before* God
[3] A vs the, *for* the   [4] if, *for* whether
[5] A lauded, demaunded, *for* laudyth, demawnd.

.S. Paul fyghtyth with the sword of the spyryt in the .xiiij. to the Corynth. And also the Prophete Esay in the .xxix. chapt., sayng :—" In vayne doth this people approch vnto me with their lyppes, their hart beyng farre awaye from me," &cete. But our shauelyngs teach, yea and command their shauelyngs, that thei be bownd to ouer ronne their seruyce, from the begynnyng to the end, and than good inowgh, wherso euer the 'hart be; but if there lacke but one verse vnsayd, thei haue a[1] grudge of conscyence and meane that all their labor is lost; for the which cause, I myselfe, in my dayes, haue sayd many tymes .ij. hundreth and fifty Aues to one Ladys Psalter, because I wold be sure to say inowe. Forsoth it may well be called lyplabor!

Our priests teach men to run over the service from beginning to end.

[* leaf 57]

Item. The Scripture teacheth what true fast is, and how to fast, in the .lviij. of Esay, that is to say; To[2] lett them out of bondage which be in danger; to breake the oth of wicked bergans; to let the oppressed goo fre; to deale thy bread to the hungry; to bring the poore fatherles to thy house; to couer the naked, &ce. For soch fast Christ offeryth us the kingdome of his father, Mathew xxv; which teacheth us also, that whan we fast, we shuld not fast to be sene of men, but vnto the father, Mathew the v.[i]. But our belly goddes teach, yea command us, a contrary fast, appoynting us dayes to absteyne from flessh. To the which fast, not only the strong, lusty, and helthy parson is bownd, but also the sycke, poore, and nedy, which hath scant nature to beare the body. And though he 'hath not eatyn a good meale in .viij. dayes before, yet must he fast their appoynted dayes. And that not only to the honor of God, but also for the honor of the sayntes, his creaturys; yea, and some also for the honor of the Pope, as the Imbryng Dayes: so loth be the bysshops that their fathers, Antichrystes, rememberance shuld

The Scripture teaches us what a true fast is;

but our Bishops teach us a contrary fast.

[*leaf 57, back]

Fasting in honour of the Pope.

---

[1] A an exceading, *for* a   [2] A To, *added.*

Where Christ teaches us to fast not to be seen of men, the Bishops will have all the world to know.

decay or be forgoten! And where as Christ techyth not to fast to be sene of me*n*, thei wyl haue all the world to knowe whan thei fast, for thei proclayme it openly alweys in the church the Sunday before, sayng:—"Such a day ye shal fast in the worshyp of this or that saynt." And yet, though he eate[1] abundance of fyssh, so that he be surfet, or drynck tyl he be dronken, thei passe not, nor their lawe reprouyth hym not. But as before is sayd,[2] though very necessyte con-

If a poor man eat a morsel of flesh on a fast day he must do penance for it.

strayne a poore man to eate a morsel of flessh vpon their appoynted dayes, he is an heretyck and must do penance. And if he wil styke to it that he may so doo by Gods lawe (as he may in dede) he shal dye therfor. Is not this a miserable thing? No man denyeth this, that if any man fele his flessh prone and ready to

[* leaf 58] Fasting is useful,

˙wickydnes, it is necessary for hym to abstayne from meates, not only flessh, but all other meates that may prouoke him to any concupice*n*ce, vntyl he hath mortifyed his flessh, and made it[3] subiect and obedyent

not on Fridays only, but every day when it is found necessary.

vnto the spiryte. But this must not be done onely on the Fryday or[4] vpon certe*n* appoynted dayes, but euery day thorout his life, whan so euer he shal fele his flessh so enclyned and bent. And this fast shal be a remedy to swage the ragyng of his flessh. And it is good to be vsed of syngle parsons, and of such as be absent from their yockfelows, & prycked to fylthynes. And

This is the fast St. Paul speaks of when writing to the Colossians.

this is the fast, which .S. Paul speaketh of vnto the Colossyans:—"Mortyfye your membres vpon erth, &c."; but to teach that[5] me*n* are bownd to forbeare or absteyne from meatys, more one partycular day than another, or more from one kynd of meate than from another (seing God hath created all to be receyued with thanckysgeuing of the*m* which byleue and know

---

[1] A haue, *for* eate   [2] A as before is sayd, *added.*
[3] A it, *added.*   [4] A on—or, *added.*
[5] A the, *for* that; B *as above.*

CH. XXIV.] THE POMP AND AUTHORITY OF BISHOPS.

the truth¹) it is a deuyllissh doctryne, as .S. Paul witnesseth, i. Tymot. iiij.

Item. Christ sayd vnto his Apostels, which were bisshops of his church, that thei shuld be ˙seruantes and mynisters, and not idols as ours be; saing:—"The kinges and lordes of the gentyles raygne ouer them, and thei are called gracios lordes, but ye shal not be so; but he that wil be grettest among yow, shal be your mynister, and he that wil be chefe, shal be seruant vnto all. For the son of man came not to be ministred vnto, but to minister vnto other." And agayne, Christ sayth;—"That foxes have holes, and the birdes of the ayer haue nestys, but the son of man hath not where to rest his head." Such possessionars were the bysshops of the prymatyue church! Now ye may openly se, that our lordly apostateys from Christ be nothing lesse than ministers or euangelical bisshops. For thei be masters, gouernors, rulers, lordes, yea and most greatest lordes. And thei wil be commyssyonars in maner in euery temporal matter. And thei be also of prynces and kynges councels, and embassytors for² princes. But woo is vnto that cyte, town, contry, or reame, where thei rule in councel! And comenly it spedeth vnhappyly to that reame, where thei be embassytors, shortly after.³ For some mischefe foloweth more or ˙lesse, or els⁴ thei fayle of their purpose, as some dyd with in these .ij. yerys, thanckys be vnto God only therfor! And whereas Christ had not where in to hyde his heade, how contrary be thei vnto hym and to his Apostels also, whose successors thei wil be called, whan thei be nothing lesse. What lordes haue more gorgyos houses than thei haue?⁵ Yea, fewe lordes lyke them. What a cockatryse syght was it to se such an abhomy-

Christ told His Apostles that they [* leaf 58, back] should be servants to His church.

He had not where to lay His head;

but our Bishops belong to Kings' Councils, and are Ambassadors.

[* leaf 59]

What lords have more gorgeous houses than Bishops have?

---

¹ A of—truth, *added.*   ² A of, *for* for
³ A shortly after, *added here, and in* B.
⁴ A or els, *added here, and in* B.   ⁵ A haue, *added.*

nable sort of pompos bisshops in lordly parlament robys as went before the king at Westmyster the .xvi.[1] day of January in the yere .1541. euyn to the nomber of .xviij. whereas .iij. were inowe to poyson an whole world. *Where such vipers are, what Reformation can be hoped for?* What godly redresse to set forth the Christen relygyon, or reformacyon of thinges for the comon welth, can there be hoped for, where such a sort of vypers be? And specially where thei beare such a swynge as Wynchester doth, to whom the grettest nomber of the bisshops do leane. How blynd be the temporal rulars styll to suffer such a kyngdome to raygne amongst them! *Everybody can see how unlike [* leaf 59, back] they are to St Paul's bishop.* Euery man may se how vnlyke thei be vnto Pawls mynd, .i. to Tymo. 'the .iij., who sayth, that a bisshop must be the husbond of one wyfe. Now it is euydent thei wil no wyues, but whores as many as thei lyst. And if any of Christes bisshops take a wife, after the second warnyng, thei will burne hym. *"Honestly apparelled," Paul says,* "Honestly appareld," sayth Paul; and how pyedly[2] goo thei lyke mommers, disgysed from the common peple. Paul *"harbourers,"* sayth, "harberos;" of whom? of the poore? No; of whom than? Of lordys, knyghtes, and men of lawe, that thei may defend their popissh kyngdom. Paul *"apt to teach." And they teach nothing.* sayth: "Apte to teach;" but thei beate,[3] & teach nothing. And if thei teach anything, what teach thei? Euen that Paul writeth of vnto Tymothe, the doctryne of the dyuel; "makyng the word of God of none effect *"Not given to lucre:" and none are such covetous wretches as they.* thorow their tradycyons." Paul sayth: "Not geuen to fylthy lucre." But where be[4] so couetos wretches in the world, as our shauelings are? He that denyeth them but one grote of that which they do but say to be their right, how will thei tosse hym in the lawe. Yea, and if he stand agaynst them,[5] thei wil serue hym as thei seruyd Master Honne, or els bring hym to the fyer.

---

[1] A xv., *for* xvi.   [2] A spiedly, *for* pyedly
[3] A beadle, *for* beate   [4] A are, *for* be
[5] A and if he stand agaynst them, *added*.

Now all men may se, that their quali'teys agree with Pauls descripcyon, as ranck poyson doth with holsom remedy. Item. The Scripture teacheth us to beare the crosse of Chryst, saing;—"Let euery man take his crosse, and folow me, &ce.;" and it teacheth us that crosse to be all maner of aduersyte and tribulacyon, which we shuld beare for the Gospels sake, after Christ all the dayes of our lyffe; as Christ saieth in the .ix. of Luke; "Who so euer beareth not his crosse dayly, can not be my disciple." And for this cause S. Paul reioyseth so oft[1] in his pistels of that crosse which he receyuyd for the Gospels sake, in the second to the Corynthyans, the .xi. chapt., Galat. the .vi., and in dyuerse other places. But our forked and open idolators teach no such crosse; but because Christ suffred death vpon a crosse (which is rotten many yeares agoo) thei wil haue men to worship all crossys, which be but symylytudes of the crosse that is rotten. And how forse thei all men to crepe vnto that[2] crosse at[2] Easter? And if thei crepe and geue no mony nor mony worth, thei shal be cownted[3] hereteyckes. Thus for lukers sake the greasy canonistes nosel the peple in 'idolatry. Oh Lord, how hast thow plaged the world for idolatry[4] and adultery! which our bisshops cannot se, because thei cannot sprytually perceyue aryght the benefyte that we receyued only in Christes blode thorow his passyon. But thei must haue a crosse of syluer and gold borne before them, which thei worship; for thei must se with their corporal eye that which thei worship. But what sayth the Scripture? "Who hath sene the symylytude of God at any tyme?" Thei wyll not beare that[5] crosse of Christ that Paul speaketh of, the .vi. to the Galathyans, but thei wil crucifye vnto death all those

[* leaf 60]

The Scripture teaches us to bear the cross,

and S. Paul rejoiced in the cross which he received;

but our bishops teach no such cross.

[* leaf 60, back]

How are we plagued for our idolatry.

Our bishops will crucify all who

---

[1] A often, *for* oft   [2] A the, on, *for* that, at
[3] A called, *for* cownted   [4] A fornication, *before* and
[5] A the, *for* that

would bear the true cross.

which wold beare that crosse. Now most deare Christyans, and specyally ye burgessys of the Parlament, here

Thus have I briefly touched—
(1) How and what Scripture teaches.

I haue brefely touched certen thinges, how and what the Holy Scripture teacheth thorow the Holy Gost, spoken and wrytten by his Prophetys, Euangelistes and Apostels, yea, and by his deare Son also, our only and ful Redemer, Jesus Chryst. Also I haue touched, as brefely

(2) How and what the bishops teach.

as I can, certen things how and what our bisshops teach, whose doctryne is as directly agaynst the Scripture of

[* leaf 61]

˙God, as Antichrist may be agaynst Christ. And, as thei agree in these fewe things, so do thei in all other. Serch the scripture, and thou shalt as easely knowe the enemies therof, as thou maist know a foxe by his furred tayle.

How can God and Mammon agree?

How can God and mammon agre? No more surely can the pompos bisshops agree with the Scripturys, because it bewrayth them. It calleth them rauening wolues in shepys clothyng, Mathew the .vij.,[1] Eze .xxij., Zophoni, iij. And do not their qualytyes in all poyntes agree

Bishops have the same pity on a right teacher as a wolf has on a lamb.

with wolues? For as lytle pytye haue the bisshops vpon a right preacher, writer, or professor of the Gospel, as hath a wolfe vpon a lambe in his hongar. There be example[s] inowe in our dayes how thei haue constrayned certen men to recant. And where as the Holy Gost sayth[2] that thei shal come in shepys clothing, do not thei come vnder the color of Gods Word, to confound both the Word &[3] Christ therto as moch as

Which are more like wolves, they who persecute or they who are persecuted?

lythe in them? I wold fayne axe a questyon; whether those that persecute, or those which are persecuted, be more lyke wolues? Thow seist that those which be

[* leaf 61, back]

persecuted, are very pore men in the ˙sight of the world (although thei be riche in God) and neyther they nor none of their doctryne neuer persecuted man vnto death. Thei haue no rule, no pour, no toth, no horne, no sword, no lawe, as bisshops haue. But the

---

[1] A viij., *for* vij.   [2] A sayth, *added.*
[3] A to confound—&, *added.*

CH. XXV.] POVERTY OF PREACHERS OF THE NEW FAITH. 73

forkyd persecutors haue vnreasonable riches, & pour of
the sword, &cc, in their handys. The pore sort¹ seke *The poor seek the blood of no man,*
the blode of no man, but are content to spend² their *but are content to shed their own*
own blode, to call³ all men vnto Christ by his word, *blood.*
with the losse of their lyues. Wherfor if thou be not
wilfully blynd, and a membre of Antychrist, thou maist
easyly se and⁴ perceyue whych be wolues & which⁵ *You may easily see which are*
lammes. The Scripture callyth them also dragons, *wolves and which are lambs.*
lyons, beares, & such other names, as in the .vij. of
Daniel, Prouer. xxviij., Ezech. xxij., and in dyuerse
other places, and all for their cruelnes, and other cor-
respondent qualyteys, which I wil no further prosecute
at this tyme, because the matter is euydent inowgh
with out any further declar[a]cyon.

A brefe rehersal, conteynyng the somme of all
that is hetherto spoken. The .xxv. Chapt[er].

NOw to touch the conclusyon of this my com- [leaf 62]
playnte; the effect (as ye may perceyue⁶) is this,
that the body of this reame, I meane the comynaltye, *The commonalty of this realm are*
is so oppressed and oueryocked, as fewe reamys vnder *oppressed by wicked laws and*
the sonne be, by wicked lawes, cruel⁷ tyrannes,⁸ which *cruel tyrants.*
be extorcionars, and oppresors⁹ of the common welth.
For all men are geuen to seke their own pryuate welth
only, & the pore are nothing prouyded for. We remayne also, and contynue styl, in a perpetual bondage
and spiritual captiutye; for as moch as we walke in all *We are still in bondage and spi-*
the¹⁰ wicked lawes, most filthy tradicyons, and beggarly *ritual captivity.*
ceremonyes of Babylon, Rome I meane, which the
bisshops of the reame (the deare childern of their father
of Rome¹¹) constrayne men, vnder the paynes of death,

¹ A sort, *added*.   ² A spede, *for* spend
³ A call, *added*.   ⁴ A se and, *added*.   ⁵ A be, *after* which
⁶ A as ye may perceyue, *added*.   ⁷ A and, *before* cruel
⁸ A tirantes, *for* tyrannes   ⁹ A and oppresors, *added*.
¹⁰ A the, *added*.   ¹¹ A the—Rome, *added*.

to obserue, by force of their inordinate riches & vnlauful auctorite. All which abuses herein mencyoned & innumerable other, which ¹I can not, neyther is it possible¹ for me to remember, for the loue that ye ought to haue vnto God, and for the hope that ye ought to haue in the merytes of Christes blode, all ye lordes, knightes, and burgessys seke, seke² to re'dresse them. And let all things be reformed, and set forth by the toch stone, which is Godds word. So that from henseforth the glory of God may be sought in all thinges, as ye haue in tyme past sought the glory of men. And where as ye haue sought euery man his own pryuate or partycular welth, now seke your neyhbors welth as your own. And where as ye haue bestowed moch ryches vpon the dead, & clothed stockes and stones, now bestow it vpon the lyuyng poore sayntes, which be the image of God as the Scripture teacheth. And let all things be done of zeale only for Gods truthes sake. And thus ye shal please God, & cause him, of his mere mercy, to withdrawe his wrath, yea, rather his iustyce, from us, that is to say innumerable plages hangyng ouer our headys & bent agaynst us, which we haue rightfully deserued, for castyng a syde Gods word and folowyng our own imagynacyons. But in case ye wil not so doo, nor harken to reforme the premysses,³ seeing God hath so many wayes warned yow (as by his mynisters, preachers, and wrytars); but wyl styll playe the Cananytes & 'tyrannys, no dowt, euen as God is God, so loke for some of the plagys of Egypt, which he wil sodenly send vpon yow, whan ye thinck least vpon them! Yea, all the examples of the Bible declare, that without diligent reformacyon & profound repentance, the reame of England, aboue all other reamys vnder the sonne, hath most rightfully deseruyd to be plaged, and that very

---

¹⁻¹ A be impossible, *for* I cannot—possible   ² A seke, *added.*
³ B nor -premysses, *added.*

shortly. For why? At this day the extorcyon and cruelnes of the temporal rulars is so come to pas, that in maner euery one of them is become a very Nero. And the yockes of the lawe be so heuy, that no faythful Christen man is able to beare them. As for adultery and idolatry, which euer stanck in the sight of God, I thinck there was neuer reame vnder the sonne, might so well be compared to the land of Sodome and Gomor as the reame of England. And further to declare the lykelyhode of your ponysshment, how hath the Word of God bene prechyd and set forth by wrytars? So syncerely, and so abowndantly, as neuer was more in any reame. And the mynisters of God in that offyce haue bene so suttylly persecuted, & so cruelly mor-*dered as was neuer more in city nor reame, no not[1] in Ierusalem, which is reproued in the Scripture for killyng of the prophetys. And all the examples of the Bible declare, that where the Word of God goth before, & is not receyued, nor no amendment of lyfe folowyng ther-upon, the plages of God folowed euer more.

Agayne. Another lykelyhode that ye shal not escape your rightful ponisshment, is this:—Many yeares past what tranquillyte hath this reame bene in, and what trobles of late hath God so fatherly pacifyed, that we might euydently se that it was his worke, and no mannys. And all to haue brought vs unto repent-ance. Agayne, what plenty of corne and aboundance of other thinges haue we had these fewe yeares past; so that all thinges had bene at a wonderos lowe price, as I think was neuer sene in Ingland, but only for that that rentys be so enhansed. Mark this, & ye shal per-ceyue, how ioyntly this[2] agreith with the .vij. fat oxen, which betokened a tyme [3] of plenty; but loke, what folowed :—vij. leane oxen, Genesis .xli. Wherfor, as

Every ruler is become a Nero.

The country is like Sodom and Gomorrha.

God's Word has been sincerely preached, and H:s ministers have been murdered.

[* leaf 63, back]

For many years we have had great tranquility; but of late what troubles has God pacified.

What abundance of corn we have had!

This agrees with the seven fat oxen and the seven lean.

[1] B nor, *for* not   [2] B it, *for* this
[3] B thing, *for* tyme

<small>[* leaf 64]
These troubles must surely come unless God turn justice into mercy.</small>

is sayd, these things be surely bent agaynst us, and must of necessity come vpon the reame, onlesse God turn his justyce into mercy. But I aduyse the, O Ingland, presume not thow there vpon, and say not but <small>O England, awake from your sleep!</small> thow art warned! Wherfor a wake from thy slepe, that thy blode come not vpon thyne oune head. The everliuyng God, who, of his iustyce, most rightuosly plaged Hierusalem, and, of his most fauorable and aboundant grace, shewyd mercy vnto the cyty of Be- <small>May God grant to the people repentance!</small> thula, that most mercyful God, grant vnto the peple of Ingland such lyke repentance as had the Ninyuytes, and to bring forth the frutes of the same, turning from their wicked wayes as the Niniuytes dyd. If thow so <small>The grace of Jesus Christ be with you all.</small> wilt, oh mercyful Lord God, so be it! The grace of our Lord Jesus Christ, the loue of God, and the felowship of the Holy Goost be with yow all: wherby ye may turne from all your abhomynacyons, to the euer- <small>Amen.</small> liuyng God. So be it, so be it!

Imprinted at Sauoy per Franciscum
de Turona.

[leaf 1] # The Lamen
tacyon of a Christen Agaynst
the Cytye of London,
for some certayne
greate vyces
vsed therin.

Psal. lxx.
Let them be abasshed and a shamed,
that seke after my sowle, let
them be put to flyght and
shame that wyll
me euyll.

In the yeare of our Lorde
M.D.XLV.

¶ The lamentacion of a Christen Agaynst the Cytie of London, & ce.

O H Lorde God, Father of mercy, and God of all consolacion, what herte can not lamente to se the Testament of thy onely Sonne, oure full and onely Redemer, Iesus Christ, thus refused & troden vnder fote! yea, all though God hathe geuen ¹oure most Soueraygne Lorde Kynge Henry the Eyght,¹ suche an hert to set yt forth with his most Gracyouse² preuyledge, yet the greate parte of these inordinate riche styfnecked Cytezens will not haue in their howses that lyuely worde of our soules, nor suffre their seruantes to haue it; neyther yet gladly reade it, or heare it redde; but abhorreth and dysdayneth all those which wolde lyue accordynge to the Gospell. And in steade thereof they sett vp and mayntayne idolatrye, and other innumerable vices and³ wickednesses of mans inuencyon, dayly committed in the Cytie of London; no⁴ reformacion or⁴ redresse ones⁴ studied for, wherby to expulse vice, and encreace vertu; nor no pol'litique inuencion for the commen welth. No, no! their heades are so geuen to seke their owne particular welthes onely, that they passe⁵

[leaf 2]

Who does not lament to see the Testament refused?

The Citizens will not have it in their houses,

they abhor it, and instead maintain idolatry.

[* leaf 2, back]

N.B. 'A' means the edition of 1542; 'B' the edition of 1548.
¹⁻¹ A *has* our kyng, *for* oure—Eyght
² A most Gracyouse, *added in this edition*.
³ A vices and, *added,*
⁴ A and, ne, not, *for* no, or, ones
⁵ A *has* not what prineledges they lose, to the great domage of the commenwelth, *after* passe

not of[1] no honest[1] prouysyon for the poore, which thinge aboue all other infidelityes, shall be our dampnacion. As apereth Math. xxv. where Christ sayth: "I was hungrye & ye gaue me not to eate; I was thurstie and ye gaue me not to dryncke; I was sicke, and in preson, and ye visited me not," &c. For not doynge these thinges shall Christe saye, " Go ye cursed childerne in to euerlastynge fyere, prepared for the deuell and his angels." Reade the text, and there ye shall se what shalbe layed agaynst you at the greate daye of the Lorde. And there ye shall also se, that ye shall not be enquired of many vayne, folishe, & supersticiouse thinges of your owne invencions, and of your popishe prestes of Baal, whether ye haue done them or not. No, no! they shalbe greatly to your dampnacion.

Oh Lorde God, how is it possible for this Cytie to expulse vice and seke after vertue, seynge they will not receaue thy Gospell, which is the worde of euerlastynge life, and that onely thinge that leadeth vs in to all truth. No, Lorde, they can not be contented, not onely to denye the receyte therof, but also the greatest parte of the seniours or aldermen, with the multitude of the inordinate riche, euen as the[2] Iewes cried out agaynst Christ, takynge parte with the highe prestes, sainge, Mat. xxvij, " Crucifie hym!" euen so doth the riche of[3] the Cytie of London take parte, and be fully bent with the false prophetes, the bishoppes, and other stronge, stoute, and sturdye prestes of Baall, to persecute vnto dethe all and euery godly person, which eyther preacheth the worde or setteth it forth in writinge (yf thou deliuer them not from their wicked snares) euen as ded their forefathers the[4] Pharisees, by

---

[1] A ne, godly, *for* not of, honest
[2] A the multitude of the, *for* the
[3] A with the greatest multitude of, *for* of
[4] B moost wycked, cruell and stonyherted Byshoppes, Scribes and, *after* the

thy seruauntes the prophetes, and also thapostels: Matth. xxiij.

O Lorde God, how blynd be these Cytizens, which take so great care to prouyde for the deade; which thinge is not commaunded them, nor a vayleth the deade, no more then the pissinge of a wrenne helpeth to cause the see to flowe at an extreme ebbe; but is the worke of mans owne inuencion & ymagynacion, accordynge to the saynge of the Prophete, rehersed[1] in Math. xiij., "In vayne worshyppe & serue they me with the inuencions and imaginacions of men." Thus follow they their owne imaginacions, prouidinge for the deade vncommaunded, & leaue prouidinge for the poore lyuinge which the Scripture most ernestly teacheth & comaundeth; as apereth in the Prophete Esay. lviij.; Rom. xiij.,[2] xv.; Luke. ˙xiiij.; Deute. xv.; ij. Cor. ix.; Prou. xxi. And that which shalbe layde to your charges, as is afore sayde, for not doinge; and the rewarde of euerlastinge life to them which, to their power,[3] haue prouyded to do for the wydowe & fatherlesse; whiche is to be vnderstonde of all pouertie, as presoner, and[4] those that be abrode.

Oh Lorde God, how is yt possible for this people to prayse the aryght, or to seke thy glorie, which, when they be in troble or plaged rightfullye of the, eyther be drught, moysture, or pestilence, or anye suche like; whiche[5] do not as the children of Israel ded when they sawe their owne iniquitye, repented & forsoke their idolatrye with all their false[6] goddes, & onely called to the Lorde God of hostes, & so obtayned? as[7] apereth in Iudicum.[8] iij., iiij., vi., x., xi., &c., & in many other

Sidenotes: These Citizens are blind in providing for the dead. | In this they follow their own imaginations, and neglect the living. | [* leaf 3, back] | Everlasting life is for those who provide for the poor. | How can they praise God aright, | who do not forsake their idolatry?

---

[1] A spoken of *for* rehersed, *and* 15 *for* xiij.
[2] A Rom. 12, *for* Rom. xiij.
[3] A for their powers, *for* to their power
[4] A as well presoners as, *for* as presoner, and
[5] A they, *for* which
[6] A vayne and falsse, *for* false
[7] A as it, *for* as
[8] A the boke of the Judges, *for* Iudicum.

places of the Bible. And seinge Christ our[1] Redemer teacheth vs in the vi. of Math., where he saith, "When ye praye, saye 'O[2] Father which arte in heauen,'" and so forth.[3] And, further, he[4] sayth also, Mat. xi., "Come vnto me all ye that laboure and are loden (meaninge with sinne) and I will refreshe you." O what a mercyfull promes is this, made to vs wretches, by hym that is all holy, all mighty,[5] all mercyfull, and will fulfill all his promises, euen as he is God alone! How madde, yea how wicked be we then, to go, to seke, to call, 'or to crye, to any other then to hym alone! Seinge he forbiddeth vs in so many places of his Holy Testament, saynge, "I will haue non other goddes in my sight. I am a iealouse God:" Exo. xx.

Marginal notes: Christ teaches us how to pray. — How mad we are to call upon any other. [* leaf 4]

But alas! these styfnecked cytizens will not come to this onelye Mediatoure, both God & man; but when they feale themselues worthylye plaged, which commeth of them onely, then will they ronne agaddynge, yea a whore hountinge after their false prophetes through the streates ones or twise in the[6] weke, crienge & callinge to creatures & not[7] the Creator,[8] wyth "Ora pro nobis," & that in a tonge which the greatest parte vnderstondeth not; vnto Peter, Paule, Iames and Iohan, Marye, & Martha, et c. And I thinke within fewe years they will (wythout thy greate mercy) call vpon Thomas Wolsey late Cardinale, & vpon the vnholy (I[9] shuld saye) Holy Mayde of Kent. Why not as well as vpon Thomas Becket? What he was I neade not to[10] wryte, it is meately well knowen. The sainge of the Prophete, Esaye. xxix., recited by Math.[11] in the xv. chapter, is verified in this people:

Marginal notes: When these Citizens feel themselves plagued, — they go to Peter, Paul, &c., — and will, ere long, go to Wolsey, the Maid of Kent, and Thomas Becket.

---

[1] A our onely, *for* our
[2] A Our, *for* O
[3] B & cet, *for* and so forth.
[4] A he, *added.*
[5] A all myghtifle, *for* allmighty
[6] A a, *for* in the
[7] B to *after* not
[8] A off the created, *for* & not the Creator
[9] A and, *for* I
[10] B *omits* to
[11] A Mathew the Euangelist, *for* Math.

"Wyth their lippes they honoure me, but their hertes are farre from me." Yea, they bete their brethe agaynst the ayre, as S. Paul saith, i. Co. xiiij., and that in vaine. Oh Lorde God, confounde them with all their false prophetes & su'persticiousnes; for they minishe thy glorie as moch as in them lyeth. What is their[1] gaddinge with "ora pro nobis"[*] vnto creatures, of them which shuld onely praye vnto the? Is it ought elles but abhominacion? No, surely! And the Cytie neuer speadeth so euell, as when they so ronne a whore hountinge. And no mervell, for they seke a wronge waye. [*leaf 4, back] *This gadding to God's creatures is an abomination.*

Oh wicked people! do not ye se that both thapostelles and angelles refused to be worshipped of men, but wold haue all the glorye gueuen to God? as apereth in the .iij. of the Actes,[2] also in the .xiiij. of the Actes, when the prestes with the[3] people of Listra wold haue done sacrifice to Barnabas & Paule. But when thapostles &[4] Barnabas and Paule harde that, they rent their clothes, and ranne in amonge the people, crienge and saynge, "Syrs, why do ye this? We are mortall men like vnto you, & preache vnto you that ye shuld turne from these vanitees vnto the liuinge God." These be thapostles wordes; reade the chapter, and ye shall see. Also S. Iohan fel downe at the fete of the Angle which opened vnto hym the secretes of God, and wold haue worshipped the Angle; but the Angle forbade him, sainge, "Se thou do it not, for I am they fellow seruaunt;" Apoc. xix.[5] Here ye se that both the Apostles & Aungles refused to be worshiped, but wold ha'ue all the glorye geuen vnto God, when they ware here vpon earth. Whether they do not likewyse nowe seke all the glorie to God & not to them selues, iudge *The apostles and angels gave all the glory to God.* *Witness Barnabas and Paul,* *and the angel which appeared to St John.* [*leaf 5]

---

[1] A this, *for* their
[2] A Actes of thappostles, *for* Actes
[3] A and, *for* with the
[4] A and, *added.*
[5] A 19 and 22, *for* xix.

thow gentle reader. And thinke ye not that if the Blessed Virgine Marie were nowe vpon earth, and sawe her Sonne and onely Redemer thus[1] robbed of his glorie (which glorie, ye blinde Citezens geue vnto hyr) wolde not she teare[2] her clothes, like as ded the Apostles? Let the godly learned iudge it.[3]

[4]Now shall ye heare what happened vnto the people of Iuda, as appereth in the .xliiij. of Ieremye, for sekinge their owne inuencions, and for offringe oblacions with their forefathers, kinges & heades, vnto the Quene of Heauen, which was the mone, temptinge the Lorde so farre, that the Lorde might no longre suffre the wickednes of their inuencions. Thus saith the Prophete : " Ye haue sene the miserie that I haue brought vpon Ierusalem and vpon all the cyties of Iuda, so that this daye they are desolate, & no man dwellinge there in ; and that because of the greate blasphemyes which they committed to prouoke me vnto angre,[5] in that they went backe to do sacrifice and worshippe vnto straunge Goddes, &c." And further more the saide Prophete saith in the same .lxiiij. cha., " Purposely haue ye set vp your good meaninge, and hastely haue ye fulfylled your owne intent." What followed in the ende? verely destruccion. Reade the ende of the same chapter, and thou shalt se.

O most dere brethern, for Christes sake geue credence vnto the Prophete, and not to the Prophete onely,. but also vnto the Holy Ghoste, which spake in the Prophete! and then loke vpon your selues, how iointly ye agre with the saide people of Iuda! They called the mone the Quene of Heauen, and ye call the Virgine Marie the[6] Quene of Heauen ; euen as the one is Quene of Heauen, so is the other. Yet be ye worsse then the

---

[1] A thus, *added*.
[2] A rent, *for* tenre
[3] A that, *for* it
[4] A Well, now, *for* Now
[5] B *omits* to prouoke me vnto angre
[6] A the, *added*.

people of Iuda. For their fautes ware written for your example. And where as they called vpon one quene of heauen, ye call vpon many. Howe many queanes of heauen haue ye in the Letany? Oh deare brethern, be no longer deceyued with the false prophetes, your bissoppes and theyr membres! Oh ye Cytezens, be ye so blynde, that ye se not that this is a blasphemy to God, and a minishinge of the honor dew to Christes bloude, to call vpon the creatures of God created? To patche and peace them with hym, as to patche the potte with the potter? And as though he ware a mercylesse God, and wold not heare but for theyr sakes. Yea & yet knowe not you whether they heare you or not, as the likelyhode is they do ˙not. For ye haue no promes of them, but of Christe ye haue. As apereth Iohan, xiiij; Mat. xvij.,[1] where he saith, "Aske and ye shall haue, seke and ye shall fynde, knock & it shalbe opened vnto yow, &c." Thus leaue ye the waye certayne for the vncertayne; ye patche him with hys creatures, because ye beleue not in hym, nor haue that faith in hym, which is of valoure before God. Yea, ye thynke he seeth not the secretes of your hertes. Oh vnwise peple, shall not he that made the hert knowe the secretes thereof? Psal. xciiij. Well, I exhorte yow, in the name of the lyuynge God, to repent be tyme, fall from your accustomed ydolatry, and leaue cryenge to your queane and[2] queanes of heauen, and call onely vpon the name of the Lorde which made all, the God of Abraham, Isaac, & Iacob; and serche the Scripture, and ye shall se how often he hath plaged the children of Israell for their[3] ydolatrye and whoredome, and all for our ensample. Repent, I saye ones againe, leste the Lorde geue you wholy vp to your owne lustes, as he dede the heithen, Rom. i., and visite you with

Marginal notes: The Jews had one Queen of Heaven—how many have you? It is blasphemy. To patch and piece God and Christ, is to patch the pot with the potter. [* leaf 6] You patch Him because you do not believe on Him. Repent, and call upon God, lest He give you up to your own lusts.

---

[1] A Matth. 7, *for* Mat. xvij.   [2] B *omits* queane and
[3] A their, *added*.

the¹ plages of Egipte, which ye haue already rightfully deserued. He is a mercifull God and suffreth longe, but when he striketh, he² felleth to the grounde.

<small>Your provision for the dead is [*leaf 6, back] more than blindness.</small>

Now to lament your blynde prouision for the deade. Alas, it is more then blyndnes 'it self; for manifestly ye³ cast Christes meretes asyde, in sekynge health for the soules of your frendes departed, by provydinge an ydle lyfe for an vnlearned prest or two of Baall; trustinge in their praier, as though these⁴ prestes had ouerplus of ryghtuousnesse more⁵ then serued them selues. Ye will saye, "No, we trust to be saued by Christes passion." I vtterly denye your truste; it is vaine and false, and without hope; or elles ye wold not seke so many supersticious waies. For Christ is the onelye waye to the Father, and is alone sufficient for all,⁶ Heb. ix. Yea,⁷ although Christe be suffycyent, yet ye will haue a prest to singe for you also, as it ware for a waretack.

<small>You say you trust to be saved by Christ—I deny it.</small>

Oh ye dispisers of the bottomlesse mercy of God, yea, whore hounters and robbers of Goddes glorie? Is Christ a peced God, or a patched Redeamer? Doth not the Scripture saye, "Ther is none other name vnder heauen wherin we maye be saued?" Act iiij.; xiij. Howe madde be ye then to seke or call vpon any other! The greate substance which ye bestowe vpon chauntries, obbettes, and such other like dregges of that abhominable whore of Rome, which most commenly ye geue for iij. causes (as ye saye) is all loste.⁸

<small>Is Christ a patched Redeemer?</small>

<small>Money for obits, &c., you give for three reasons.</small>

Fyrst, that ye will haue the seruice of God mayntayned in the churche to Goddes honoure; and yet by the same seruice is 'God dishonored, for the Supper of the Lorde is peruerted and not vsed after Christes institucion: Math. xxvi.; Marc. xiiij.; Luc. xxij.; i. Cor.

<small>1. You will have God's service maintained, [*leaf 7]</small>

---

¹ A part of the, *for* the
² B *omits* he
³ *Orig.* y
⁴ A the, *for* these
⁵ A in them, more, *for* more
⁶ A for all, *added*.
⁷ A Yee, say ye, *for* Yea
⁸ A is all loste, *added*.

xi.; and so is that holy instytucyon¹ turned into a vayne supersticious cerimoniall Masse (as they call it) which Masse is become an abhominable idoll, and of all idolles the moste greatest; and neuer shall ydolatrye be quenched, where that ydoll ys vsed after Antichristes institucion: Daniel ix.; Math. xxiiij.; whiche no doubt shalbe reformed, when the tyme is come that God hath apointed, euen as it is vsed already in diuerse cyties of Germanie.² Yea, although all the Antichristes in the hole worlde wolde saye the contrarye, and all their disciples with them; yea, although they studie to set all the princes of the earth to gether by the eares, to let that and soche lyke godly redresse, as it is their olde cast; yet he sitteth in heauen that laugheth them to scorne, and he shall make their wisdome folyshnes: i. Cor. i.

but the Mass is become an idol, and of all idols the greatest,

and God shall laugh you to scorn.

The seconde cause is for redeamynge your soules and your frendes, which is also abhominable. For who soeuer will seke redempcion, iustificacion, saluacion, or to be made righteouse by the lawe, he is gone quite from Christ, and hys merites profyte hym not. Reade the thirde chaptre to the Romaynes, and the iiij. to the Hebreues, the iij. to the Galath., and also Esaye. liij., 'i. Cor. i., and there ye shall see. Perchaunce ye wyll saye, ye seke no soche thynge thereby? Oh ye vnwyse, and open dissemblers, wherfore then do ye it? Ye saye lyke as the idolatoure nowe adaies doth, yf he set a candle before an image and idoll, he sayth he doth not worshippe the image, but God whome it representeth! For (saye they) who is so folysh as to worshippe an image? As who shulde saye, none. I answere, wherfore doth God in so manye places of the Scripture, forbidde vs to worshippe idolls or images, as Exo. xx.; Deut. v.; Sapi. xiij., xiiij.; and throughout all the

2 It is for redeeming souls; this also is abominable.

[* leaf 7, back]

You say, 'If I set a candle before an image, I don't worship it.'

Why does God forbid the worship of idols?

---

¹ A memorye, *for* instytucyon
² A *has* as Zurich, Basyll, and Strasz- burg, and soche other &c., *after* Germanie.

Prophetes, but that he knewe that¹ ye wolde worshyppe them with your forefathers? Euen so ye, bycause ye haue not full trust in Christes meretes, ye grope after vayne waretackes. If thou wylt set a candle before the image of God, thou must be diligent daylye to helpe thyne neyghbour acordinge to thyne estate; which thinge I haue towched before.

He knew you would follow your forefathers.

The iij. cause of your good intent is, that the profites of your goodes maye come to the prestes, as though they ware the peculyar people of God, and onely beloued; as in dede to those whiche preache the Gospell, be the people bounde to geue a² sufficient lyuynge. For the workman is worthye of his rewarde, Math. x.; i. Tim. v. But not that their prayer can helpe the ·deade, no more then a mans brethe, blowynge in the sayle, can cause a greate shippe for to³ sayle. So is this also become abhominacion, for those be not Christes mynysters, but the mynysters of a rable of vncommaunded⁴ tradicions and popishe ceremonyes. And ⁵thus ye be the maynteyners of⁵ a sorte of lusty lubbars, which be well able to laboure for their lyuynge, and stronge ynoughe⁶ to gett it with the swete of their faces, as the Scripture teacheth them: Genesis iij.; i. Thesa. iiij. And thus be ye mayntayners of their ydlenes, & leaue⁷ the blynde, the lame, & the presoned vnholpen, whiche the Scripture commaundeth you to helpe;⁸ except it be on the Sondayes with a fewe halppens, or by ꝑeany meale, which helpeth lytle or no thynge. But vnto⁹ those blynde guydes ye will geue, vi., vij., viij.; yea xij., poundes yearly to one of them, to synge in a chauntrye, to robbe the lyuynge God of his honoure.

Ye will saye vnto me, "What arte thou that callest

S. You intend the profits of your goods to come to your priests.

Their prayer can't help the dead.
[* leaf 8]

You maintain lusty lubbers (who could get their own living)

and leave the blind and lame without help.

---

¹ A that, *added.*
² A a, *added.*
³ A to, *for* for to
⁴ A dyrtye, *for* vncommaunded
⁵⁻⁵ A ye fynd, *for* thus—of
⁶ A ynoughe, *added.*
⁷ A leaue the syck, *for* leaue
⁸ A *has* (The places be afore recyted) *after* helpe
⁹ A vnto, *added.*

these thinges vncommaunded¹ tradicions and popishe ceremonies, seynge the Kynges Grace forbiddeth them not, and vseth parte of them hym selfe?" I answere that ye vse manye thinges contrary to the kyngs iniunccions. And yf it be so² that God, through the kynge, hath caste out the deuell out of this realme, and yet both he and we soppe of the broth in which the deuell was soden, and that God hath yet not opened the eyes of the kinge to set all thinges in right frame, and vtterly to breake downe the serpent, as Ezechias the kynge dyd, iiij. Reg. ix.; and as kinge Aza dyd, ij. Chro. xiiij.; take it thus, that euen your inyquitye with callynge vpon vaine goddes, & sekinge saluacion by a wronge waye, is the very cause that God closeth vp the eyes of the kynge, as of one that³ heareth and vnderstandeth not, and seeth and⁴ perceyueth not. *[You will say—The King uses some of these things himself. [* leaf 8, back] We drink the broth in which the devil has been sodden. Your iniquity causes God to blind the eyes of the King.]*

But for the reuerence of Christes meretes,⁵ where as ye haue walked some in verye symple ignoraunce, and some in obstinate or wilfull ignoraunce, and groped in tymes paste after a wronge waye, derke, croked, harde, and endles; now seke the ryght, trew, & onely waye which is light, streyght, and easy to fynde, that is to say, Christ the onely Messias, and redresse these thinges, easy to be done. Turne your chauntries and your obbetes from the profite of these berewolues whelpes, whiche can neyther helpe the soules of your frendes departed, nor yet yours, after God hath taken you from thys lyfe; & scripture ye haue none to encorage you but only your owne inuencyons; & against you are places innumerable, and specyally, Rom. xiiij., where the Apostle sayth, "Whatsoeuer is not of fayth is sinne." Your chauntries and ceremonies are without Godes worde, and so must they be without fayth; ergo they *[Turn your charities from these whelps who cannot help you, [* leaf 9]*

---

¹ A dyrtye, *for* vncommaunded
² B *omits* so
³ A that he, *for* as of one that
⁴ A but. *for* and
⁵ A merytes sake, *for* meretes

be sinne. Bestowe them therfore from hence forwarde vppon the trew image of Christe, which is vppon the poore, the sycke, the blynde, the lame, the presoner et c. Oh ye Cytezens, yf ye wolde turne but euen the profytes of your chauntries and your obbettes to the findynge of the poore with a pollitique and godly prouision ! where as now London, beyng one of the flowers of the worlde as touchinge worldlye riches, hath so manye, yea innumerable of poore people forced to go from dore to dore, and to syt openly in the stretes a beggynge, and many not able to do for[1] other, but lye in their howses in most greuous paynes, and dye for lacke of ayde of the riche, to the greate shame of the, oh London ! I saye, yf[2] ye wolde redresse these thinges, as ye be bounde, and sorowe[3] for the poore, so shulde ye be without the clamor of them, which also crieth vnto God agaynst you, and which he well heareth ; and then, where as now ye haue an houndreth extreme poore people, shall not be one ; and in so doinge your owne goodes shall not be a witnesse agaynst you at the greate day of the Lorde, as it wilbe against your forefa'thers for not prouydinge for the poore. Besydes that, what a ioye shall it be, to se your bretherne well prouided for !

Ye abvse your riches, specially you that come to thoffice of the Cytie, for ye spende vnmeasurably. Vppon whome ? Euen vppon them that[4] haue no neade ; as vppon the nobles and ientlemen of the courte ; vppon the aldermen and other riche commoners, whiche haue as greate neade of your[5] feastes as hath the see at the highest of the springe tyde, of the pissynge of the wrenne ; [and] the pore forgotten, except it be with a few scrappes & bones, sent to Newgate for a face ! Alasse,

---

[1] A ere, *for* for
[2] A If saye I, *for* I saye yf
[3] A prouyde, *for* sorowe
[4] A which, *for* that
[5] A your great, *for* your

alasse! how lytle it is, the Lorde knoweth! I thinke
in my iudgement, vnder heauen is not so lytle prouision
made for the pore as in London, of so riche a Cytie.
Well, the poore well feleth the bournynge of Doctor *Dr Barnes urged you to look upon the poor.*
Barnes a*n*d his fellowes, which laboured in the vyne-
yarde¹ of the Lorde. For accordynge to there office,
they barked vppon you to loke vppon the poore, so
that then some relefe they had; but now, alasse, ye be
colde; yea, euen those whiche saye they be the favorers
of the Gospell! It is a token that your foundacion was
buylded vpon the sande, for that God hath suffred your
prophetes to be brente.² Though they be gone, considre it was not their commandemente,† but³ Goddes, †*Orig.* com-
whose Testame*n*t ye haue in⁴ your very 'mother tonge, mnademente.
thankes be to the Lorde therfore! In the same ye [*leaf 10]
may perceyue that their absence shulde not quenche
nor mollifye your loue towardes your⁵ brethern. And
doubt not but God shall rayse other that shall speake *Doubt not God will raise up others with a like spirit.*
with the same sprete that they dede, & with no lesse
loue & vehеmen*c*y; if your⁶ yniquytie be not cause to
the contrarye. There is a custome in the Cytie, ones
a yeare to haue a quest called the warnmall queste, to
redresse vices, but alasse, to what purpose cometh it,
as it is vsed. If a pore man kepe a whore besides his *If a poor man keep a whore he's punished.*
wife, & a pore mans wyfe play the harlot, they are
punisshed as well worthye. But let an Alderma*n*, a
ientlema*n*, or a riche man kepe whore or whores, what
punishme*n*t is there? Alasse, this matter is to bad!
I saye some of your Aldermen kepe whores to the
greate shame of all the rest. Yt weare no shame to
name the*m*. Wherfore repent & amende, or surely I *It were no shame to name the alder-men who do so.*
will, yf God lende me lyfe, in an other worke name you,

¹ B *omits* in the vyneyarde
² A *or rather* morthered, *after* brente.
³ A the very lyuyng, *after* but
⁴ B euen now in, *for* in
⁵ A your poare, *for* your
⁶ B *omits* your

and other of your affynyte,[1] which be openly knowen to be common aduouterers; which is no lytle shame to the heades, and other rulers of the Cytie, to suffre such abhominacion. But no maruell though ye suffre bodely aduoutrers, seinge ye your selfes are spyrituall aduoutrers, callyng vpon vayne godes. Ye will saye I sclaundre you and brynge[2] vp false lies vpon you.[3] Some of you knowe whether I sclaundre you or not.[4] I wold it ware a sclaundre. But I sclandre you so that, except ye repent and amende your lyuynge, as well ye that be sufferers of such vices, as the committers; except ye amende, I saye, and seke redresse of this and such lyke, the vengeaunce of God will lyght vppon the cytye for your synnes. For howe can ye do iustice vpon a nother and ye offende in the same your selfe? Yea, and how parciall be ye that punishe the pore, and leaue vnpunished those heades that[5] shuld geue goode example to the rest? Awake, awake! for the Lorde slepeth not, althoughe ye thynke that[6] he wincketh at this gere. I exhorte you in Godes name, loke better in[7] chosinge of your heade officers. Let not riches only cause men to rule; and specially loke better to the[8] chosinge[9] your officers of the lawe. Howe can dronkardes, whoremongers, & couetouse persons geue ryght iudgment? Do briers bringe forth figges, and thorns grapes? And, I saye vnto you, the parcialyte of iudges, suppressynge the pore, &[10] aidynge the riche for lucre, and in condempnynge the innocentes, and lettinge the wicked go fre, bryngeth the vengeaunce of God vppon all places; as appereth in Esay. iij. Here I coulde saye sumwhat

Side notes:
- This is a disgrace to the City.
- [* leaf 10, back]
- Except ye repent, the vengeance of God will come upon you.
- Choose better officers, and better judges—
- their partiality against the poor
- brings God's vengeance upon all places.

---

[1] A Jentellmen of the Courte, *for* of your affynyte

[2] A He sklaundereth that bryngeth, *for* and brynge

[3] A vpon you, *added.*

[4] A I had almost saide that halfe or all the bentche shall knowe at the last daye that I saye trueth, the moare pitye it is, *after* not.

[5] A which, *for* that

[6] A that, *added.*

[7] A vpon, *for* in

[8] A on in, *for* to the

[9] B of *after* chosinge

[10] A in, *for* &

ALL BISHOPS OF LONDON INFAMOUS. 93

more then I nowe will, I meane in[1] condempnynge the[2] innocentes.

'Thinke ye that God hath not as moche to laye to the charges of London for killynge hys seruantes, as he had against Ierusalem for killing the[3] prophetes? Yes, yes. For Godes sake, ye that be elders, repent and geue your selfes to readinge the lawe of the Lorde, that ye maye be an example to the conmons (sic) in Godly conuersacion! And in the Scripture ye shall lerne what to do, and what to leaue vndone, and howe to knowe false prophetes, & howe[4] to cast them out of your consciens, where they haue sytten a[5] longe tyme, euen in the stede of God. I meane not the Bisshope of Rome alone, but he and all his marke with hym, and specially his owne generacion, which are all in[6] forked cappes. [*leaf 11] *Give yourselves to reading the law of the Lord.*

What a plage is this, that in no mans tyme aliue, was euer any Christen bisshoppe rainynge ouer the Cytie of London, but euery one worsse then other. I thinke their can now come no worsse, except the same Lucifer that fell from heauen, come hym selfe, whiche is the very father of all popishe bisshoppes! Considre thys is for your iniquitye. Yet let the litle flocke reyoice, and geue God onely thankes, that he hath raised other meaner membres in the syght of the worlde then bisshoppes to preach the Gospell, and to set it forth in wrytinge. *There never was a Christian Bishop in London; there could be no worse except Lucifer himself.*

Now to all you, though ye be fewe in nombre, which fououre Godes Holy Worde vnfaynedly, and not in worde onely, but in workes also,[7] shewynge the frutes of your faithe, say I thus,—exhortinge you for Christes bloude sake to be dilygent in prayer, onely to the euerliuynge God, that he, of his owne mere mercy, geue [*leaf 11, back] *You who favour God's word, be diligent in prayer,*

---

[1] A concernyng the, *for* in
[2] A of, *for* the
[3] B hys, *for* the
[4] A wherby, *for* howe
[5] A of, *for* a
[6] A in, *added*.
[7] A specially those commaunded in the scripture, *after* also

grace to the rulers of this Cytie, that from henceforth they maye seke Godes glorye onely, the common welth, and prouisyon for the poore. And then, doubt ye not, but God shall geue our noble Kynge suche a*n* harte that he shall knowe, and soche eyes that he shall plainly see, and soche eares that he shall vnderstonde in deade. For why, it is the Lorde that hath the hert of all princes in his hande: Pro. xxi. So that, I saye, where as he hath now bannisshed out of hys realme but the very bearewolfe the whore of Babilon onely,[1] shall now also bannish with her all her folishe[2] tradicions, & beggerly ceremonies, agaynst whiche S. Pau. wrote ad Galata. iiij, and in many other places mo. Now shall your[3] papisticall sorte dispyse this my lamentacion, a*n*d laugh me to scorne. Although I knowe there is no Christen herte in this realme, no nor in the whole worlde, whiche knoweth the vices vsed in the[4] Cytie, & how lytle Godes glorye is sought, how lytle the commone welth is sett by, howe baerlye the poore are prouyded for, but he wyll lame*n*t with me. And as for the contrary par'te,[5] I wysh with all my hert repentaunce, & will continuallye, my lyfe duringe, praye vnto the euerlyuinge God, to drawe them to the Gospell of his sonne Iesus Christe, and that they maye come to the Father, by the onely waye & dore, Christe; & that they may also[6] forsake their bydores, & clyminge in at the windowes, wherby they shall neuer atayne to any sauinge helth. [7]O Lorde God, I beseche the,[7] call them from that no*m*bre whome the Almightie syttinge in heauen laugheth to scorne: Psal. xxi. The only cause that I wryte

then God will bless our noble King,

so that he shall banish both the whore and her traditions also,

The papists will despise my lamentation,

[* leaf 12]
but I wish them repentance,

and will pray God for them.

---

[1] A and yet gnaweth vppon her dyrtye tradicyons with vayne and folish ceremonies made by the whore and her abhominable predecessoures, *after* onely

[2] A fylthy, *for* folishe

[3] A the, *for* your

[4] A this, *for* the

[5] A to be auendged apon them, *after* parte

[6] A also, *added.*

[7-7] A nether by the Masse of Scala coeli, of the 5 woundes, ner by no other soche lyke tromperye, and I praye God, *for* O—the

this, is to exhorte all men, as well readers as hearers, to repent betymes, and to fall diligently to prayer; askynge mercy, that we maye auoyde the plages which we rightfully haue deserued, & no doubt we shall not escape them all, onles we repent the soner. Remember how he warned the cytie of Ierusalem, xl. yeares longe; and because they repented not, but slewe the prophetes by whom God warned them, he kept promes with them and scourged them accordynge to their deseruinges. And he that spake the same to Ierusalem speaketh it to yow & to all cyties that committe like iniquite as ye do.[1] And whether ye haue serued the disciples of the Lorde, like as dede the cytezens of Ierusalem her[2] prophetes, iudge your selues, & ye shall se that ye haue shed more bloud then euer dede that moste synfull[3] Ierusalem, ˙euen of them that taught you Godes truth. Well, I can no more; but besche the Lorde God, that he will geue suche grace to some, that in the tyme of his wrath he maye finde x. righteous persons in this Cytie, whereby the wrath and vengeaunce of God maye be turned from it; which is lyke to come shortly vppon vs, or vppon our childern, for our sinnes and our forefathers. For we haue deserued a thousand tymes more plages then euer dede Tire and Sidon, or Sodoma and Gomorra. Ware it not for the greate mercy of God, I thinke we had founde it so or this time. For we haue an example of these cyties, and they be written for our learninge to avoyde suche vices. Yea, no doubt the vices committed in the, oh London, are as euell as euer ware in any of the foure cyties afore named. And surely I thynke, yf they had herd the preching that hath bene in London this xiiij. or xvi. yeares past, that

I write to exhort all to repent betimes.

Jerusalem was scourged according to its deseruings.

London has shed more blood than Jerusalem.

[* leaf 12, back]

May God find ten righteous men in it!

We deserue more than Tyre and Sidon.

If they had heard the preaching London has,

---

[1] A and ye haue bene warned lyke as was Jerusalem almost this 20 yeares, yee and moare playnely ar warned than euer was Jerusalem, or any other Cytye that euer was afore oure tyme, if ye marck well all thinges, *after* do.

[2] A his, *for* her; B their, *for* her

[3] A that most synfull, *added*.

they had repented.

they had repented and forsaken their inyquitye. For I saye vnto you that the Gospell was neuer more sincerelye preached in the tyme of the Apostles then it hath bene of late in London; nor neuer more godlye exposicions vppon the Scripture, and that a greate nombre, whereby to drawe vs to Christ Iesus. For

The Holy Ghost speaks to us,
[* leaf 13]

why, the same Sprete, euen the very Holye Ghoste, which spake in the Apostles, hath spoken in men now to vs.

but we hear not.

But alas, as the Prophete sayth, Isay. xxix., "We haue eares and heare not, eyes & see not."

See ye not, nor yet perceyue ye,[1] how the blynde prophetes haue led you, euen now in our tyme? Haue

You have slain the Lord's servants.

ye not slayne the seruauntes of the Lorde, onely for speakynge agaynst the authoritye of the false Bysshoppes of Rome, that monstruouse best, whom now ye your selues do, or shuld, abhorre? I meane all his lawes, beynge contrary to Christ, and not his body; and yet ye se that a fewe yeares past ye brent them for heretiques abhominable, which preched or wrote against his vsurped

Now it is treason to uphold the Pope's power

power; and now it is treason to vpholde or mayntayne any parte of his vsurped power; & he shall dye as a traytoure that so doth, & well worthy. So saye I vnto you, there shalbe yet thinges preched vnto you, and ye shall be instructed by wryters of thinges which ye be not

Yet here are preachers still who shall die.

yet able to beare, and whosoeuer preacheth or writeth it (if the Lorde defend him not out of your handes) he shall[2] dye for it. And yet out it will at the lenght, though all the deuelles in hell saye naye to it; and so shalbe reformed. And euen this followynge is one of the chefest thinges.

Will you never read the Scriptures?
[* leaf 13, back]

Oh ye Cytezens, will ye neuer geue your selfes to the readynge of the scrip'ture, whereby ye maye knowe the lawe of the Lorde, to avoyde the euerlastinge damp-

---

[1] A ye, *added.*   [2] A must, *for* shall

nacion, which is ordayned for the deuell and his angles? Wyll ye euer be ignorant of Godes commaundement, Exodi. xx., saynge ;—"I will haue non other Gods in my syght, and that ye neyther bowe your selfe, nor serue any thinge as God, that is in earth benethe, or in heauen aboue, or in the water vnder the earth?" And do ye not yet se how this whore of Babylon hath altered the Supper of the Lorde which was instituted to haue the b[l]essed Passion in continuall remembraunce, & for[1] a perpetuall memorye of thankes geuinge? which we shuld receyue with all reuerence and meaknes of hert, geuinge tha*n*kes vnto[2] God onely for that benefyte which we haue receyued, and obtayned through Christes dethe, which this Supper sygnifyeth ; and that we beleue, as verely as we eate the breade & drinke the wyne, which norisheth the body & is seane with our corporall eye, and spiritually representeth the very body of Christ ; euen so, verely, as we haue tasted, eate*n*, and seen this Holy Supper or Sacrame*n*t of thankes geuynge ; euen so verelye to beleue that Christ dyed for our sinnes, and that his bloud onely hath pacyfied the Fathers wrathe,[3] and so hath sett vs at peace with God. For he hath payed that which laye not in me nor in no man, but onely in hym that was bothe God & man ; and by none other meanes might man be redemed ; and so to acknoweledge that he is dede, & hath shed his bloude for our synnes, and is rysen for our rightwysnesse.

Thus I, seinge my synnes buried in Christes woundes, must euer more be tha*n*kfull to the euerliuynge God onely. And thus to eate his blessed body and to drynke his bloude spyritually in fayth, is Goddes institucyon. Math. xxvi. ; Marc. xiiij. ; Luc. xxij. ; i. Corinth. xi., where he sayth, "As ofte as ye shall eate of this breade

Will you ever be ignorant of God's commandment?

The whore of Babylon has altered the Lord's Supper,

which we should receive in all meekness.

As we eat the bread and drink the wine, we ought to believe that Christ died for our sins.

[* leaf 14]

To eat Christ's body and to drink His blood spiritually, is God's institution.

---

[1] A to, *for* for
[2] A to the lord, *for* vnto
[3] A wrath of God the Father, *for* the Fathers wrathe

and dryncke of this cupppe (*sic*), ye shall shew the Lordes dethe till he come."

S. Austin says, believe, and thou hast eaten,

And saynte Austyn sayth, "What preparest thow they tethe and thy belly? beleue and thow hast eate*n*." Which agreeth with the wordes of our Sauiour Christ, saynge : "The fleshe profiteth nothynge, it is the spryte that quyckeneth :" Iohan in the vi. chapter. But the institucion of Antichriste is cleane contrary to this. For by his institucion thow muste fall downe vppon thy knees, holdinge vp thy handes as to God. In dede it is the Bysshoppe of Romes[1] God which they must see with their corporall eye, because they haue no hope in the lyuynge God, through the spyrituall eye.

but the Church of Rome is contrary to this,

[* leaf 14, back] *and the memory of Christ's death is changed into the worshipping of bread.*

And thus hath he chaunged the holy 'memory of Christes death in to the worshippynge of his God made of fyne flower; and all to bringe him selfe and his membres alofte, and in the reputacion of the worlde, aboue all degrees of men, yea, aboue Kinge and Emperour; and therby to sitt in the consciences of men, aboue God and his worde, euen in the very temple of God, where God alone shulde sitt. And by his institucion of this his God, is he crept vp in to this his vsurped power.

Oh Antichrist, the begynner of this idoll, which is the[2] heede of all idolles, after thyne institucyon, doth not God saye, as afore is sayde, Exo. xx., "Thou shalt not worshippe any similytude that is in heaue*n*, erth, or in the waters vnder the earth?" And thou, contrary to the euerlyuinge Goddes commandement, hast seduced the people to honore thy god. I tell the, gentle reader, ones agayne, it is the greatest idoll vnder heauen as it is vsed in his Masse, and a God of the makynge of Antichrist, as is sayde; whiche Masse is, [3]after his institucyon, an heape of[3] folishe ceremonies without signi-

God says, Thou shalt not worship the likeness of anything.

The greatest idol under heaven is used in the Mass, and a god of Antichrist's making.

---

[1] A Popes God and his membres. For he and they must and wyll haue a, *for* Bysshoppe of Romes

[2] B *omits* the

[3-3] A dyrtye dregges and, *for* after —heape of

ficacyons, to avaunce and sett out his God, to the blear-
ynge of the eyes of the simple.   And thou shalt see, if *In the Revelation you will see the trash which has been sold to us;*
thou wilt reade the xviij. chapter of the Apocal., call-
ynge to God onely to open thyne eyes, all the trishtrashe that Antichrist hath solde vs, whiche¹ be the
onlye² 'implementes of the Masse of Antichrist; I [* leaf 15]
meane not the Antichrist of Rome onely, but also of all *not by the Roman Antichrist only, but all Antichrists.*
other popysshe By[s]hoppes,³ with all their brethern in
Antichrist. And in the sayde xviij. chaptre thou shalt
see the fall, not onely of the whore alone, but also of
her merchaundyse, the⁴ same tryshtrash with her. For
euen as the whore is fallen in Englond already, thankes *The whore is fallen in England.*
onely be geuen to God therfore, and yet her trishtrash
remaynynge for our iniquities sake, euen so, I saye, in
the sayde xviij. chaptre thou shalt see that her mar-
chaundyse must followe, when the tyme is come that
God hath appoynted.   No doubt our vnthankfulnesse *We were vnthankful, and gave glory to men, and not to God.*
sake, & the geuynge of glorye vnto men, which shulde
be geue*n* onely vnto God, is the cause of the longe remaynynge of the premisses. The wordes of the xviij.
chaptre⁵ be these :—" Alas, alas, the greate cytye Babi- *Isaiah says judgment is come upon Babylon,*
lon, that myghtie cytie, for at one houre is her iudge-
ment come. And the merchantes of the earth shall wepe *and the merchants will weep, because no man will buy their wares.*
and wayle in the*m* selues, for no man will bye their ware
any more ; the ware of golde, and siluer, and precious
stones ; nether of pearles, and raynes, and purple, and
skarlet, and all thynne woddes, and⁶ brasse, and yron,
and sinamom, & odours, and oyntmentes, and fraken-
cense, and wyne, and oyle, and fyne flower, and
sowles of men. This fyne flower haue they made 'the [* leaf 15, back]
chefeste of all their trishtrashe, and a cloke or a cloude

---

¹ A trish-trash, *after* which
² A the onely, *added*.
³ A wynchester, of london, of dyrr-
ham, Salisbury and worceter &c, *for*
all other popysshe Byshoppes

⁴ A that, *for* the
⁵ A of the Apoca., *for* chaptre
⁶ A all maner vesselles of lucrey,
and all maner vesselles of most pre-
cyous wood, and of, *after* and

to shadow all the reste. Rede the chapter and thow shalt perceyue more.

<small>Pardons have been sold</small>

I praye the ientle reader, iudge; ware not the pardoners merchantes to them? Yea, it is well knowen that their pardons, and other of their tromperye, hath

<small>in Lombard Street as horses are in Smithfield.</small>

bene bought and solde in Lombard Strete, and in other places, as thow wilt bye and sell an horsse in Smithfelde. Yea, and at Easter, when thow shuldest come to the Supper of the Lorde to receyue the sacrament of thankes geuynge, there muste thow receyue the God of Antichrist without significacion or godly instruction.

<small>You must pay for Antichrist's God.</small>

Yea, and thou must bye it, and paye for it, as men somtyme bought[1] pyes in Soper Lane. Yea, and thou must paye for his God or thou haue it. Yea, I haue harde of pore men, for lacke of two pens, been[2] put from receyuynge of their God; and, for lack of paynge the parson or vicare his dewtie, many haue been put from it.

<small>Christ's body cannot be eaten.</small>

And more I tell the reader, that the bodye of our Sauiour Iesus Christ, can not be eaten with teth, it must be eaten with faythe, as is a fore sayde.

<small>That which has beginning or ending cannot be God.</small>

And further, marke this well,[3] that thinge that[4] hath begynnynge or endinge can not be God, nor ought to be worshypped as God.[5] So can this Sacrament no more be

<small>[* leaf 16]</small>

'God then was the paschall lambe. For God is without begynnynge and endynge; and so is not the God of Antichriste; for he is made manye tymes be a synefull ipocryte.

Well then, it hathe a begynnynge, and maye perishe

<small>A mouse may eat the bread; the wine may stink.</small>

and moulde awaye; and the litle mouse will eate it, if he maye come by it. And the wyne wyll waxe sower and stincke, as doth their holy water in the founte by longe kepinge; whiche hath bene the destruction and deth of

---

[1] A twopeny, *before* pyes
[2] A *omits* been
[3] A well, *added.*
[4] A which, *for* that
[5] A nor—God, *added.*

innumerable childern; where as two or thre droppes of water taken out of it by the prestes handes, and cast vppon the childe ware sufficient, and the childe neuer neade to be taken out of his clowtes. Now to my purpose agayne. *Death in the font.*

Oh thou blynde man, can the body of Christ perishe by any maner of meanes, as to waxe sower, or that any maner of bestes maye eate the bodye of Christe? No surely, God forbidde! [1]For he (as concernynge his Godheade) was from the begynnynge, and shall be with out endynge. As manyfestlye it appeareth in Iohan the first chapter:—"The worde was in the begynnynge with God, &c."[1] But this marke well,[2] that euen as the passeouer lambe was a sygne, a token, and a remembraunce, to put the childern of Israell in memorye of their corporallye,[3] or bodelye ˙delyueraunce, and also that Messias shuld come to be slayne for their sinnes, paynge their raunsome, and delyuerynge them from euerlastinge dethe; which moued the faythfull of them to be thankefull to God, for that they beleued, as verely as they dede eate of the lambe which they had slayne; euen so verely had God delyuered their forefathers from the plages whiche fell vppon the wicked vnbeleuers; and also that a Redemer shulde come, whiche God the Father had promised, by the mouth of his Prophetes. And thus dede they bothe eate Christes bodye and drynke Christes bloude, in fayth spyritually, many yeares afore Christ was borne. Euen so the Sacrament of thankes geuynge is to vs a sygne, a token, a spirituall memorye of our spyrituall delyueraunce. For the faythful beleueth [4] euen as verelye as they [5] see and eate it, so do they acknowledge the benefytte *Christ's body cannot become sour.* *As the Passouer was a sign* *[* leaf 16, back]* *of deliverance to the Israelites,* *so the Sacrament is a sign of our spiritual deliverance,* *and the faithful acknowledge the benefit.*

[1–1] A *from* For—God, &c., *added*.
[2] A well, *added*.
[3] A corporall, *for* corporallye
[4] A euen as verely as they receaue
this holy sacrament of thanckesgeuyng, *after* beleueth
[5] A both, *after* they

THE LORD'S SUPPER IS A SACRAMENT OR SIGN.

which they receive in the holy Sacrament.

which they receaue in and throughe the immortall God, and which the same holy Sacrament representeth; & no doute the very body of Iesus Christ is spyritually in and with vs in the receyuynge of the Sacrament, if it be resayued with the fayth afore sayde; euen lyke as he is amonge two or thre which be gathered together in his name, as it is his godlye promes, Math. xviij.

The same faith which saues us [* leaf 17] saued the old fathers,

Thus ye maye se that the same fayth which saueth vs, saued the olde 'fathers; for they beleued, through that outwarde sygne, that a Redeamer shulde come, and we, through the memory of thys holy Sacrament of thankes genynge, beleue that he is come, and hath fullfylled all that was of hym prophesied. And thus bothe they and we eate the holy body of Christ spyrituallye in one fayth.

who ate the body of Christ spiritually in one faith.

And farther, vnderstonde, reader, that vnto all beleuers the ceremonye of eatinge the paschalle lambe ceassed immediatly when Christ had chaunged it in to a maundaye of thankesgeuinge. For why the next daye was fullfilled, by the death of Christ, that thynge whiche the paschall lambe to them dede represent.

If it is a Sacrament, it is a sign of some holier thing than itself.

Thou sayest it is a Sacrament, which I bothe graunt and write. If it be a Sacrament, as it is in dede, then it is a sygne of some holier thinge then it selfe is. And beynge a sygne of a holier thinge then it selfe is, so can it not be God; for what sygne or token wilt thou haue holier then God? None. Ergo, then it is not God him selfe, but some sygne, token, or remembrance of some benefytte whiche we haue through him; and this holy sygne putteth vs in remembrance of the same[1] to be thankfull to the Lorde.

What sign or token can you have holier than God?

Thou wilt saye it is God hym selfe, euen flesh, bloude, and bones, yea and senewes therto; as[2] Master Standish, one 'of your wyse false prophetes, preached of late amonge you; but yet denye I that, for all his vngodly

[* leaf 17, back]

[1] A thereof, *for* of the same   [2] A wyse, *after* as

learninge. For how can it be a sacrament of God and It cannot be a sacrament of God, and God Himself. God him selfe also, seinge there can be nothinge holier then God? And agayne if it be God that is present, thou foole, what neadeth the of anye sacrament or signe of that thinge which is present it selfe?

As touchinge this matter, Iohon Fryth, the seruaunt John Frith has written on this matter: of the Lorde, whom ye & your false prophetes haue burned, whose bloude with others cryeth vengeance againste your bysshoppes:—He, I saye, hath writen invyncibly in this matter; whose worke I exhorte all I exhort you to read his work, those whiche fououre the free passage of the Gospell vnfaynedly, to reade and to studye. For it is agreynge to[1] the touch stone, Godes Worde, and to the olde auncyant doctours, as appereth by the same boke of his. And I exhorte you, in Godes name, yf there be anye Christyan printer in London, to prynte moo of those workes,[2] and to print more such. for there can neuer be to many of them.

Feare not man although death followe, seinge Christ sayeth, "he that loseth his lyfe for my wordes sake shall saue it:" Mathewe in the xx. chapter.[3] And considre that neyther Winchester, nor London, nor the rest Neither Winchester nor London can destroy more than the body. of the bysshoppes,[4] the vesselles of Godes iustice, without repentaunce, `haue no power to destroye but the [* leaf 18] bodye onelye; wherfore feare them not. But feare hym onelye that can kyll both bodye and soule, as appereth in the same xx.[5] chap. For if thou wylt lyue godly in Christe, thou muste neades suffre persecucyon. And truly he is not worthy to be a membre of the body, that wyll suffre no dyspleasure with the heade. Ther- Blessed are they that suffer persecution for the sake of Christ. for blessed are they that suffre persecucyon or anye trobble for ryghtousnes sake; that is for Christes sake.

And in this matter I saye with the sayde Iohon

---

[1] A unto, *for* to
[2] A that worck, *for* these workes. B those, *for* these
[3] A Matth 10, *for* Mathewe—chapter.
[4] A pysspottes, *for* Bysshoppes
[5] A 10, *for* xx.

Fryth, that it is no pointe of our dampnacion nor saluacyon. If[1] I beleue it not, it dampneth me not. But to haue the absence of the benefyttes of his deathe and passion in my hert, maye be cause of my dampnacion; and in beleuynge of the sayde benefytes, of and through his dethe, shalbe my saluacion, beinge repentaunt for my synnes.

But one thynge I will tell the, and marke it well, for it is trewe. Though thou beleue he is there like as Antichryste and his petye membre Standishe saythe, and so worshippe it as God, I tell the that it is dampnable. For thou arte commaunded in the fyrste Table of the commaundementes, that thow shalt not worshippe anye thynge that is made after[2] anye symylytude or lykenes[3] that is in heauen or earth, as I haue afore sayde. God is a sprete, and wilbe honored in sprete and veryte. I saye your blynde and bloudy bysshoppes, or rather butchers, dishonour not onely the Sacrament, but the God of all goddes also, in mynistrynge the same. And so do all prestes, that other synge or saye the popishe Masse, which they call a sacryfyce, & therby wold haue Christes bodye daylye crucyfyed[4]; where as he offred vp his holy body vppon the crosse for our synnes ones for euer, and neuer shalbe offred agayn, while the worlde endureth; but hath instytuted the Holye Supper, or Sacrament of thankesgeuynge, as afore is sayde, to put vs in contynuall memory of that oblygacion and sacrifice, that we shuld beleue our synnes to be forgeuen onely for Christes sake, through his death, and so to be thankfull: which holye thynge, as ye se, is turned in to a popishe Masse, and is to the people a domme, yea, a deade ceremonye.

Sidenotes: Frith's opinion. — If you believe God is present in the Sacrament, — it is against God's command. — [* leaf 18, back] — Bishops and priests dishonour God in the Mass. — It is a dumb ceremony.

---

[1] A If I beleve he is there flesh and bloudd and bonnes etc. it saueth me not nether if, *for* If
[2] A of, *for* made after
[3] A or lykenes, *added.*
[4] A sacrificed, *for* crucyfyed

GIVE UP THE ABOMINABLE BLASPHEMY.

Wherfore I will exhorte all prestes that wylbe of Christes congregacion, to fle and geue ouer that abhominable massynge, which is a blasphemy to Christes bloude, in that they make of it a sacryfice. What sacrifice can that be where no bloude is shedde? Wherfore in Christes name, all yow, I saye, that wolde be of Christes churche, forsake thys whore with all her ˙abhominable rabbles, and rather begge with Christ, then welthelye to lyue with the prestes of her god Beell; and feare not, but God shall prouyde both clothynge and foode suffycient for the bodye.

Considre the lylye dothe not spynne, yet was Salomon neuer so gorgyouslye apparelled: Mat. vi. Who clothed the lylye, dede not our heauenly Father clothe it? And be not ye worth manye sparowes? Well, then, we see that our[1] heaue*n*ly Father both clothed[2] & fedde[2] all creatures; a*n*d shall not he also clothe and feade yow, which seke his glorye, & trust onely in hym? Yes, yes, doubt not. And surely ye can not remayne as ye do, but ye muste be partakers of ther idolatrye.

Perchaunce thou wilt saye, 'I could be conte*n*ted to lyue porely to follow Christe, but I feare the byshopes blessyng, which is a fayre fyre.' Set afore the the deth of Christe for prechinge his Fathers will, and before hym the Prophetes, and after hym his Apostles, and at thys daye hys chosen seruauntes, and considre, as afore is sayde, that the deuyllyshe byshoppes,[3] the vesselles of Godes iustyce, can but destroye the bodye onelye, and that God will rayse it vp agayne at the greate daye of the Lorde, euen as surely as he[4] is rysen. And considre, that alwayes it was the bisshoppes and the highe prestes that put ˙Christ and[5] his Apostles and his chosen seruauntes to deathe. And by their deuellyshe

I exhort all priests to give over saying mass,

[* leaf 19]
and rather beg with Christ than live wealthily with the priests of Baal.

Shall God not clothe and feed you?

But you may fear the bishops' blessing.

They can only destroy the body.

The bishops and high priests put Christ to death.
[* leaf 19, back]

---

[1] B pure, *for* our
[2] fdede *in orig*. A clotheth, feadeth
[3] A deuelles pispottes, *for* deuyllyshe Byshoppes
[4] B *omits* surely as he
[5] A and, *added*.

sedusynge, euer blynded the prynces and other heade rulars to geue their consent ther vnto: Math. in the xxi. and in the xxvi. chapter.

O ye generation of vipers, where does your authority come from?

O ye Babylonyshe bysshoppes, and[1] generacion of vypars, where haue ye your auctorytye, or how dare ye be so bolde to kyll a man for his fayth; which Christ neuer ded, nor hys Apostelles? For it is a gyfte which no man can eyther geue an other or yet hym selfe. No, no, it is the gyft of God onely.[2] And that must be geuen a man before he can eyther do or thynke goode. For all that is done without fayth is synne: Roma. in the xiiij.[3] and Hebre. xi.

Bishops put men to death because they should not preach Christ.

No, nor ye put no man to death for Christes sake, but for that that no man shulde eyther preache, teache, or wrytte Chryst aryght; whiche he can not do,[4] but he shall by force be constrayned of the Holye Ghost to wryte agaynst your pompe, pryde, vyle lyuynge, and agaynst your abhomynable sedusynge of the people, leadynge them in an endlesse mase of dyrtye tradicyons and folyshe ceremonyes.

Why can't a man set forth Christ?

[* leaf 20]

It is because he must speak against your false bishops.

And why can not a man set forthe Christ but he must wryte agaynst yow? Euen bycause ye be the verye Antichry'stes. No, I saye it is not possible for anye man, sent of God, eyther to preache or wryte,[5] but he must open his mouthe agaynst[6] Antichriste, as agaynste[7] the enemye of Christ, whiche be you false bysshoppes, false prophetes, that beare the false sygne of the new lawe & the olde lawe;[8] with stoute, stronge, & sturdye archedeacons, deanes, and chanons of cathedrall churches, and other your pyty membres, prestes of Baall. And he that openeth not his mouthe agaynst

---

[1] A I wyll commen a word or two with your Busshoppes O, *for* O—and.
[2] A *has* Jam. 1, *after* onely
[3] B xxiiij, *for* xiiij.
[4] A which he cannot do, *added*.
[5] A preacher or wryter, *for* to—write
[6] B that moost wycked abomynable and detestable Antychryste of Rome, *for* Antichriste
[7] A which is, *for* agaynste
[8] A lawe, *added*.

you, can not truly set out Christ; a*n*d that is the cause why ye seke their deathes.

Ye bewitche kinges and other rulers, and turne their laboures, I meane the laboures of the seruauntes of God, whiche crye agaynst your iniquyte, saynge they teache sedycyo*n*, & cause rebellyon agaynst the hygher powers. {*You bewitch kings and rulers.*}

Oh ye childerne of Satan, all that reade their workes maye beare recorde with them agaynst your lyes. Who teacheth so moche the obedyence towardes the hygher powers, as God onely in the*m* doth, which preache or wryte the Gospell? Yea, hath not God through their preachynges,[1] brought your[2] kyngedome vnder the temporalle powers, which many yeares hath vsurped ouer the*m*?[3] And, bycause ye wolde not be vnder the obedyence whiche the Scrypture teacheth, hath coste manye a 'thousande mens lyues, and some prestes amonge. And this poynte I wyshe vnto all kynges, that will not willfully be blynde, to beware of yow crafty and wylye bysshoppes. Although they wyll not considre the iniuryes that they haue done to Christes churche or congregacion, in persecutynge them vnto dethe for truly preachinge and writynge Godes glorye, and mynishynge the glorye of Antichrist; although, I say, that the kynges of the earth and other high powers wyll not consydre Christes cause, yet let them co*n*sydre theyr owne, what & howe tyrannously the bisshoppes kyngedome hath vsed their progenitours, Kynges of Englo*n*de? Agaynst whome they ware euer the heades a*n*d the begynners, the[4] foundacion and the very orygynall of all mischeue. Reade the storye of Wyllyam Rufus, and of Kynge Henry the Secounde, howe he was vsed by Thomas Becket; Kynge {*You children of Satan, all who read bear witness against your lies.*} {*God has brought you under the temporal power.*} [* leaf 20, back] {*Let all kings beware of bishops!*} {*I would have them remember how tyra*n*nously they have behaved.*} {*Read how Henry II. was used by Becket.*}

[1] A preachers, *for* preachynges
[2] A your wycked, *for* your
[3] A ye haue not bene, *for* hath— them
[4] A ground and, *after* the

EVIL DEEDS OF THE BISHOPS.

and how the good King (!) John was used by Langton.

Iohon, howe he was vsed of and by Sthephen Lanckton, Bysshoppe of Cantorbury, whiche wyll pytye any Christen herte to heare, as well for the wycked vsynge of the goode Kynge, anoynted of God, as of the bondage and thrauldome[1] that he brought the whole realme in. But suche is the charytye of the[2] bysshoppes as well in all other realmes where they maye beare rule,. as in Englond.

[* leaf 21]
Some of the kings' troubles came from Abbots,

'And though it appere that some of the trobles which chaunsed to the Kynges of Englond, in tymes past, came by Abbotes of these fylthye monasteryes, ryghtfully deposed nowe of late,[3] yet came the grounde from the[4] forked marchauntes. For be thou sure, neuer came any displeasure to anye Prynce in Englonde or elles where for sekynge any godly redresse and[5] Goddes glorye; but the orygynall and mayntayners of the same ware these forked cappes. Aboue all the membres of Antichrist, I saye, beware of them, all you that wyll not wyllfully be blynde. They be the verye ryght and chefe wolues that Chryst speaketh of, Math. vij, callynge them "wolues in sheppes clothynge." What is that sheppes clothynge? No doubt the Worde of God, vnder the pretence of the which worde they come to confounde the[6] worde as moche as lyeth in them. Their actes appere to them that will not willfullye be blynded. Full well knowe they, yf they shulde not come vnder a pretence of holynes, and speciallye with a[7] pretence of the Worde of God, of the churche of God, of the doctryne of Christ, of the olde true learnynge, of seauen or eyght[8] hondreth yeares olde & c.; that no man wolde beleue them. Yet for all their outwarde meakenes and holynes, they be within

but most came from Bishops,

who are the "wolves" spoken of by Christ.

They come with a pretence of holiness,

and of the true learning,

---

[1] A thraull, *for* thrauldome
[2] B *omits* the
[3] A a late, *for* now of late
[4] A these, *for* the
[5] A and sekyng, *for* and
[6] A that, *for* the
[7] A the. *for* a
[8] A 15, *for* seauen or eyght

THE KING'S INJUNCTIONS SET AT NOUGHT.

rauenynge wolues, accordinge to Christes saynge in the place aboue rehersed, as their actes and charytye hath appered, of late¹ yeares, vppon the seruauntes of God. And Christ here sheweth vs howe we shulde knowe them. Reade the places, and ye shall see them descrybed, as appereth i. Timot. i. and ij. and ij. Timot. iij. and i. Iohan. ij. and iiij. And, yf ye will geue no credyte to it, your owne bloude vppon your heades, accordinge to the sayenge of of the Prophete Ezechiell in the iij. chapter.

[* leaf 21, back]
but they are only ravening wolves.

If you will not believe it, your blood be upon your own heads.

How is this to be lamented, seynge the kynges grace hath set out iniunccions, that all vycars, persons, and curates, shall purely, and syncerely preache the Gospell, and leaue their owne dreames; and yet, not with stondynge these iniunccions, whoso euer preacheth the Gospell aryght, but euen the verye text whiche the Holye Ghost wrote, and cryeth agaynste the callynge vppon any sauynge helth through the wayes and worckes of mans inuencions, agaynst the which all the Prophetes crye, as is afore sayde; he, I saye, that so truly laboureth in the vineyarde of the Lorde, ye bysshoppes wyll eyther hange hym, or bourne him, or pryuelye murther hym. And vppon² the contrarye parte, let them neuer so openly preche there owne dreames, yet maye no man troble them, nor saye black is there eye. And no mar'uell, for Christ hath promysed them no troble or crosse in thys worlde,³ which preache not, but persecute hys worde.

The king enjoined the gospel to be preached,

but if a man labour truly to do so,

the bishops burn him.

[* leaf 22]

Thus be ye theues and robbers of all Chrystyanytye, stealynge from vs the spyrituall foode of our soules. Yea, a thousande tymes worse be ye then the thefe that robbethe vppon the hygh waye for neade. And yet so bewytche you the hygher powers and the riche of the worlde, that they can not escape⁴ your robberye; &

You are all thieves and robbers, stealing from us our soul's spiritual food.

¹ A a late, *for* of late
² A vppon, *added*.
³ A as, *before* which
⁴ A espye, *for* escape

no maruell, for the worlde wyll loue hys owne, as Christ sayth : Iohan. xv.

You have so bewitched the parliament by your inventions,

O ye deuelles, ye blynde guydes and seducers of the people, howe of late[1] bewytched you the Parlament house? Euen by your inuencions and deuelyshe studye, haue ye caused actes and decrees to be made, so cleane contrarye to the lawes of the lyuynge God, that I saye vnto you, the[2] verye bearewolfe, that abhomynable whore of Rome, neuer made so cruell actes. He neuer made it dethe for a preste to marye a wyfe. But ye shame not onelye to seperate them that be maried, so contrarye to Godes Worde, whiche saythe, "Let no man seperate that whiche God hath coupled," Math. xix, but[3] haue also[3] made it deathe.

that it has made it death for a priest to marry.

Paul says let every man take a wife.

[* leaf 22, back]

Peter had a wife, as is plain to be seen.

Oh generacyon, worse then the vypar. Dothe not Saynte Paul saye, "Let euerye man that hath not the gyfte of chastytye take his wife," i. Cor. vij. Here is no parson excepted. And that the Apostles had wyues the Scripture is playne. As saynt Peter wyth other,[4] Math viij.[5] Ye wyll saye, 'ye haue the gyfte of chastytye.' Well the chastytie of the moste parte of you, that[6] procured those wicked actes is meately well knowen, and therfore make ye it no abhominacion to kepe whores. Ye abhorre the remedy ordayned of God, and mayntayne the remedy of sathan, as appereth by Wynchesters gardyn. Well ye bysshoppes, and ye chanons of the churche of Beell,[7] ye shutters vp of Godes Worde, accordynge to his owne prophesye, Math. xxiij. Luc. xi., to you I can saye no more, but, though the worlde or worldlye people laugh vppon you, yet wyll the vengeaunce of God lyght vppon your forked cappes and[8] cathedrall churches of Beel one daye ; & that

You abhor the remedy God has provided,

and God's vengeance will come upon you.

[1] A alate, *for* of late
[2] A that, *for* the
[3] A yet, ye, *for* but, also
[4] A wyth other, *added.*
[5] B viiij., *for* viij.
[6] A which, *for* that
[7] A these cathedrall churches, *after* Beell
[8] A your, *after* and

shortelye, exccpte ye amende¹ betymes. Ys not your auurycular confessyon also abhomynable? Yes, and that one of the moste fylthyest thynges vsed vppon earth, as hath playnlye appered by the feates of your chaplaynes in diuerse places of Englonde of late,² and some within thys two yeares.³ I coulde name the prestes and the⁴ places also; but I will passe it ouer with sylence, trustinge in the Lord, the hygher powers shall ones so the mischefe that commeth therof and redres͘se it. What an abhomynacyon is it that I shulde go poure out my vyces in⁵ the eare of an vnlearned buzarde, and specyally for a woman, whereby Syr Iohan knoweth where to be sped. Yea, if⁶ she will not graunt to hym, he will not shame to threaten her to open her vice, and so for feare she must agree to his abhomynable desire.

Auricular confession is abominable,

but I will pass over it in silence.

[* leaf 23]

Why should I pour my vices into the ears of the ignorant?

What a blyndnes is it to thynke my sinnes forgeuen me, when a prest of Antychrist (as the most parte be) hath wagged two or thre fyngers ouer my head? Dauid sayth, "I confessed my synne vnto⁷ the Lorde, and he harde me and forgaue me," Psal. xxxij.⁸ The Israelites, when they had offended the Lorde God, and after ernestlye repented, callynge to the Lorde onelye for mercye, brynginge forth the⁹ frutes of repentaunce, ware in contynent deliuered from their aduersaries; as appereth, Iudicum .viij. ix., and in manye other places of the Byble.

It is blindness to think when a priest has wagged his fingers over my head my sins are forgiven.

Israel confessed its sins to God and was forgiven.

Thys was before anye auriculare confession was knowne. For that no dout was the inuencion of Antichrist of Rome. And one chefe cause was to betraye princes, and other greate men. For what noble man was it in Christendome that spake agaynst forked cappes

Confession was invented to betray princes.

¹ A repent, *for* amende
² A alute, *for* of late
³ A this yeare, *for* within—yeares
⁴ A the, *added*.
⁵ A into, *for* in
⁶ A and, *for* if
⁷ A to, *for* vnto
⁸ B xxii., *for* xxxij.
⁹ A ther, *for* the

112   REASONS AGAINST AURICULAR CONFESSION.

[* leaf 23, back]

All this is manifest enough in England.

manye yeares longe, but the bysshoppe of Rome had his confession with all speade, and sodenlye they wolde[1] bewitche the prynce of the[2] ʻrealme, and fordge some matter agaynst hym, and so of force he shulde be made a traytoure, and so suffre dethe. I thynke thys matter be manyfest ynough to manye men, as well in Englond as elles where. Well, this vyle thinge was not from the begynnynge, neyther shall it contynewe to the ende. Euen as your inordinate possessions ware not of your[3] heauenlye Fathers plantynge, and therfor muste be plucked vp by the rotes, with youre companyons and bretherne in Antichryste, Abbottes, as is afore sayde.

Confession can't be well used while priests live as they now do.

Some wyll saye it maye be well vsed, whiche I vtterlye denye. It shall *nor* can *neuer* be well vsed, so longe as prestes maye kepe whores without daunger of dethe, whiche burthen maye rightfullye be layde vppon them, seynge they abhorre matrymonye instytutede of God ; agaynste whyche synne was no remedye but dethe in the olde lawe, where as thefte was but rendrynge double. For this and soche lyke thynges, "Be ye lerned ye rulers, lest the Lorde be angrye:" Psal. secundo.

If I repent and intend to avoid my old sins,

[* leaf 24]

I am forgiven for Christ's sake.
If I am unrepentant, all the priests in England cannot pardon me.

Agayne I saye it shall neuer be well vsed of all prestes, as[4] longe as they shall grope our partyculare synnes, whiche is not necessarye. For why, yf I be repentaunt, and ernestelye mynded neˑuer to fall to myne accustomed synnes agayne, I doubte not but I am forgeuen, without the preste, for Chrystes sake onelye. And yf I haue not that repentaunce, euen from the bottome of my herte, and beleue not that I am forgeuen for Christes sake, as is[5] afore sayde, all the prestes in Englond, saye I, nor yet the beare wolfe of Rome, can forgeue me. Thus ye maye se

---

[1] A so, *after* wolde
[2] A that, *for* the
[3] A our, *for* your
[4] A so, *for* as
[5] A is, *added*.

wherein consysteth͏e confessyon for the offence to Godwarde.

And as touchynge thy neyghboure, thou must reconsyle thy selfe to hym whome thou hast offended, and make restytucion to thy power; and yf thou be not able to make recompence with goodes, thou oughteste to offre hym thy bodye. And euen as thou arte bounde so to do, so is he bounde to shewe the mercy. But do[1] thou thy dewtye, and thus euerye neyghboure to reconsyle oche to other, is the right confessyon[2] chaunsynge betwene brethern or neyghbors, as apereth in Iohan the vij. chapter,[3] and in Mathwe. the vij.[4] chapter.

I must be reconciled to my neighbour.

To make restitution and do your duty, is true confession.

Thou bysshoppe, and[5] thou false prophete, wilt say that it is ordayned of God, and wilt brynge in chefely for the, that Christe sent the tene lepers to the prestes. Whiche serueth asmoche for[6] confession, whiche we make to a preste,[7] as to 'laye an ynyon to my lytle fynger for the tothe ache. To you blynde guydes, that be ignorantly blynde, speke I, and not to these that be willfully blynde. Let them be still blynde; yet I exhorte all Christians to praye for them that they maye see. But wilt thou knowe the trewe causes why Christ sent those lepers a boue all other which he healed, and none other to the prestes, reade the .xiij. and the[8] xiiij. chapter of Leui. : and there shalt thou see that it was appoynted of God, that no parson, ones hauinge the leperye, shuld come amonge the congregacion of the whole, till he was clensed. And for a certainte that he shulde be first whole, the prest had the ouersight, and kept hym certayne dayes for a tryall, to be sure that he was whole, before he wolde so admitte hym. And

The bishop will say confession is ordained of God, and refer to the lepers, healed by Christ.

[* leaf 24, back]

But they were sent to the priest only to fulfil the law;

the priest had charge of them for a time,

---

[1] B *omits* do
[2] A for offences, *before* chaunsynge
[3] A James 5, *for* Iohan—chapter
[4] A Matth. 5, *for* Mathwe—chapter
[5] A and, *added.*
[6] A auriculer, *after* for
[7] A which—preste, *added.*
[8] A the, *added.*

when the prestes founde him whole in dede, then dede they admitte¹ hym, after he had offred the oblacion commaunded in Moyses lawe, to go abrode amonge the whole; and for bycause Christ wolde not breake the lawe, but was the fullfiller of the lawe, sent he them to the prestes, not to shewe their synnes (for they shewed none duringe the hole tyme of Moyses lawe) but for the cause afore sayde. An other cause that he sent them was, that the prestes sclaundred Christe, sainge that he blasphemed: Math. ix., Luc. v., Iohan. v. Therfor Christ bad them ⁎offre the oblacyon commaunded in Moyses lawe, ²for a wytnes vnto them; yea no doubt² for a witnesse agaynst their infydelytie. For they of³ force must confesse that Chryst healed them. For why, they admitted them for cleane and receyued the oblacyon, and yet sclaundred they Christ, so settynge them selues without all excuse of their moste worthye and wyllfull dampnacion.

Christ dede not onely sende the tene lepres, but also other lepres that he healed. But let them fynde that euer Christe sent anye other that he healed to the prestes, as the sycke of the palseye,⁴ the diseased of the blouddy flyxe, the possessed with deuels, and soche other like, whiche notwithstondynge ware synners as well as the lepers, and had neade of⁵ remission of their synne⁶ as well as they, then let me dye for it.

O ye Antichristes, ye your selues maye see howe lytle this text of the lepers serueth for aurycular⁷ confession. Woo be to⁸ you, ye wresters and wrythers of Goddes holy worde; I coulde bringe in as goode authoritye agaynst the reste of your wycked decrees, but I wyll differ⁹ it to the makynge of an other worcke,

---

¹ admttie *in orig.*
²–² B *omits* for a—doubt
³ A a, *for* of
⁴ A palsey syck, *for* syck of the palseye
⁵ A neaded, *for* had neade of
⁶ A of their synne, *added.*
⁷ A or eare, *before* confession
⁸ A vnto, *for* to
⁹ B defer, *for* differ

THE KING ADVISED TO PLUNDER BISHOPS. 115

which shall be shortelye,[1] yf the Lorde lende me lyfe. Yf not, I doubt not but he shall rayse other that shall accomplyshe that which I˙haue begonne. For doubt not but Godes chosen wyll, withe the Scripture, fyght agaynste your wycked decrees, yea although their bloude be shedde therfore. Yea,[2] as moche ioye haue they to set forthe the glorye of God, and to brynge their brethern to the knoweledge of your blynde errours, and to teache them the waye to avoyde them, callynge them to Christ; euen asmoche ioye, I saye, & with as free a herte, as ye haue to robbe Christ of his honoure, geuynge parte to hym, parte to the creatures by hym created. Yea and moche more then ye haue in mayntaynynge of your kyngdome in pompe and pryde, and in shedinge of the bloude of innocentes. For we knowe that the Lorde hath promised vs none other rewarde in this lyfe. And ye haue made wonderous goode prouisyon for the same. For who soeuer shall preach Chryst or write Christ aryght, he is incontynent in the net eyther of fellonye, treason, or hearesye, or in all thre. But at the grete daye of the Lorde, at the rysynge of all fleshe, ye generacion of vypars shall se that those shalbe founde faythfull bothe to the kynge of the bodye onelye, and also to the Kynge of bothe bodye and soule. And then ye shall be founde in deade fellons, traytours, and heretyques, both agaynst God and man; and soche wyll ye be so longe as ye posses˙se your[3] inordinate riches, that wycked Mammon.

God gene the Kynge an hert to take that wycked Mammone from you, as he maye ryghtfullye do with the consent of the commones by acte of Parllament; so that it maye be disposed to Godes glorye and the commone welthe. As to take hym selfe a porcyon[4] for

I have another work which will soon be ready.

[* leaf 25, back]

God's chosen delight to set forth His glory, and show up the errors of Rome.

If a man preach Christ aright, he is in the net of felony, treason, or heresy.

At the last great day he shall be found faithful.

[* leaf 26]

May the king take your riches from you, as he has a good right to do,

---

[1] A I wyll make, *for* shall be shortelye
[2] A Yea and, *for* yea
[3] A that, *for* your
[4] A as 8 or 10 of euery hundreth, *before* for

a knowledge of obeysaunce, and for the mayntaynynge of his estate. The rest pollytyquely to be put vnto a commone welthe. Fyrst distributed amonge all the townes in Englond in sommes accordynge to the quantyte & nombre of the occupyars, where moste neade is. And all the townes to be bounde to the Kynge, that his grace[1] maye haue the money at his[2] neade to serue hym.[3] And also a pollytyque waye taken for prouysion for the pore in euerye towne, with some parte to the maryages of yonge parsons that lacke fre*n*des. Wayes there are ynoughe, who so lusteth to studye for them.

Yet one thinge wolde I wyshe to[4] all me*n* if it ware Godes pleasure; that is,[4] that all men wolde take you, euen as ye be[5] forked cappes, wherof the Apostels neuer ware any, ye bysshoppes, ye false prophetes, for euen[5] as the vypar aboue all other[6] wormes or serpentes is most fullest of poyson for cartayne† qualytyes in hym; 'euen so ye, aboue all the membres of Antichriste, be the moste fullest of poyson, swiftest to shedde bloude, the greatest persecuters of Christes congregacion, yea, & ye haue euer done most myschefe in shuttynge vp of Godes worde from the people, aboue all other knyghtes of the Rome[7] churche. Well, your wycked Mammon, your inordynate ryches, was not of our heauenlye Fathers plantynge; therfore it muste vp by the rotes, with the ryches of your other brethern of the Romishe churches,[8] or church malygnant, whiche of late ware ryghtfully plucked vp.[9]

[1] A so that he, *for* that his grace
[2] A his extreme, *for* his
[3] A he rendryng it agayne, *after* hym
[4] B *omits* to all men—is
[5] B are, that is euen lyke, *for* be forked—for euen
[6] B beasts, *before* wormes
[7] B romysh, *for* Rome
[8] A church, *for* churches

[9] A *has, after* plucked up:
I wold to God the distribucyon of the same landes and goodes had bene as godly distributed, as the act of the roatyng vp was, which distribucyon, I darre saye, all Christen hertes lament. For the fatte Swyne onely were greased, but the poare Shepe to whom that thing belonged had least or nothyng at all. The faute wyl be

TREACHERY OF BISHOPS AGAINST KINGS.

If thou wylt reade the storyes of the thre kynges aforesayde, thou wylt saye it is hyghe tyme to pull from them that wycked Mammon. In the same stories ye shall see what knaverye hath euer bene practyzed of the bysshoppes, aboue all other impes of Antichrist, as well agaynst the¹ kynges, as agaynst the preachers, teachers, and writers of Christes Gospell, moste lyke² vnto the vypar, as afore is sayde. Vnderstonde also what the propertye of the³ vypar is: she destroyeth her make or male in the concepcyon, and the thynge conceyued (I meane the ionge in the lytterynge, or forth bryngynge) dest[r]oyeth the damme. So bysshoppes, whome kynges make Lordes of beggers, be commonly the fyrste that procure them displeasu're; as appereth by the storyes of these kynges afore sayed. Yea, they haue put mo kynges to troble then euer came to lyght. For why it must neades be trewe that Chryst sayeth of them :—" The childern of this worlde be wyser, in their generacyon, then the childerne of lyght be in theirs."

What thynke ye of the insurreccion of⁴ the Northe? Surelye in my iudgement (I wyll speake no farther) it was their⁵ inuencyon, & they⁶ ware the⁷ grounde and foundacyon ⁹therof. It is as well possyble for the sonne to be without lyght, as that this shulde be wythout truthe, that the bysshoppes ware the causes⁸ therof.⁹ Well, though¹⁰ Chryst sayethe, " ye be so wyse in yower generacion," yet makethe it not agaynst these wordes,

Read the stories of William II., Henry II., and John, and see what knavery has been practised.

The viper destroys her mate, and her young destroy her.

So do bishops, whom kings have made lords.

[* leaf 27]

They have given kings much trouble.

I think the insurrection in the North was their doing.

layed to all those of the parliament house, specially to those which beare the greattest Swynge. I touche this matter here, to exhort all that loue Gods worde vnfaynedly, to be diligent in prayer onely to god, to indue the lordes, knyghtes, and Burgeses of the next parlement with his Sprete, that the Landes and goodes of these Busshoppes may be put to a better vse, as to Gods glorye, the welth of the commonaltye, and prouysyon for the poare.

¹ A the, *added.*
² A lykest, *for* lyke
³ A & B a, *for* the
⁴ B *omits* the insurrection of
⁵ B but it was their owne, *for* it was their
⁶ B the Bysshopes, *for* they
⁷ B very orygynall, *before* grounde
⁸ A causers, *for* causes
⁹⁻⁹ B of the same Insurrectyon, uproare and tumulte, *for* therof—therof
¹⁰ B although, *for* though

that your wysdome wyll proue folishnes, i. Cor. i. Which God graunte maye be shortlye, that the pore selye lambes maye preache & teache the Gospell, and that the rest, which yet be wythout, maye espye your dysceyte, and fle from your dyrtye tradicyons, and followe their owne Shepherd, whiche so louynglye gaue hys lyfe for them.

May the Gospel soon be preached!

I knowe the papystes and their flocke shall sclaunderouslye report me, other to be[1] agaynst the Sacrament, which am dyrectly with it, after Christes institucion, & full agaynste the instytucion of the Rome 'bysshoppes, as ye shall perceyue yf ye marke and pondre my sentence aryght; or elles they wyll saye, I am an Anabaptyste, whiche opynyons of them that are agaynste the Scrypture (as they haue dyuerse) I vtterlye abhorre, whiche opynyons neade not here to be touched.

I know the papists will slander me about the Sacrament,

[* leaf 27, back]

or else will say I am an Anabaptist.

Your olde crafte is also to sclaunder vs, saynge we be causers of insurreccyon; in whiche poynte euen as I therin nowe shall shewe my mynde, so haue all those done which[2] laboured in the vyneyard, of whome ye haue bourned a greate nombre. I acknowledge and geue to vnderstonde to all that shall eyther reade this my[3] Lamentacion,[4] or heare it redde,[5] that all kynges and rulers haue their aucthorityte & powers of God, & whosoeuer resysteth[6] them, or those whiche of them be sent, resysteth God, Rom. xiij., and so seaketh his owne dampnacyon. Yea, although a kynge be a tyraunte, we maye not resyste hym. Yea, and further,[7] although a kynge shulde be so wycked to make actes or lawes euen dyrectlye agaynste Godes lawes, as dede kynge Darius, Danyel vi., and also the hyghe prestes and

I acknowledge that all kings have their authority from God.

Although a king be a tyrant,

---

[1] B that I am, *for* other to be
[2] A haue, *after* which
[3] A my pore, *for* my
[4] B worke, *for* Lamentacion
[5] A or heare it redde, *added.*
[6] B they that resist, *for* whosoeuer resysteth
[7] B *omits* further

Pharisees forbyddinge Peter and Iohan to preache Christ, Actu. iiij. ; yet maye we not wyth fyst and swerde, & ce., resyste them, nor be auenged of them, no more then dede Daniell and the other childern resyste Darius ; 'or Iohan and Peter, the prestes and Pharisees, or Christe Pylate : Mathe. xvi.[1] *we may not resist him with any kind of weapon.*

[* leaf 28]

But, gentle reader, marke, that euen as we maye not resyst them wyth fyste, swearde, or weapon, & c., but to owr dampnacyon, euen lyke wyse maye we not obserue their wycked lawes, nor consent or agree vnto them with hert or mouthe, vnder payne of the selfe same dampnacyon ; but rather suffre deth, then eyther to resyste them bodelye wyth[2] strenght of hande, or consent and agree vnto their wycked lawes and actes in hert or mouthe, after the example of Daniell, Christ, the Apostles, Prophetes, Martires, & ce. ; and after the example of the mother wyth her seuen sonnes :[3] Machabe. vi. Whych example is wrytten for our learnynge, with many suche lyke. *Nor may we obserue wicked laws, but rather suffer death, as did Daniel, Christ, the Apostles, Prophets, and Martyrs.*

And marke this, that euen as all subyectes be bounde to the hygher powers, and to be ruled by them in all thynges, as lawes, decrees and suche other, grounded vppon Scripture, & not to[4] resyste in[4] payne of dampnacyon ; so muste the hygher powers be ruled by the Scrypture, and make no lawes contrarye to the Scrypture, in[4] payne of lyke dampnacyon vnto them. For that is the onelye touchstone, whych tryeth all thynges, and whych muste gouerne all thynges. *The higher powers must be ruled by Scripture.*

Thus I ende my Lamentacyon, beseachynge God, through his Sonne[5] Iesus 'Christ, to drawe you from all *Thus I end my Lamentation,*

[* leaf 28, back]

[1] A 26, *for* xvi.
[2] A with force or, *for* wyth
[3] A 2 Macha. 6.
[4] A to, in, in, *added.*
[5] A *has, instead of the words* Thus —Sonne, *the following :*
Thus I ende, beseching the God of peace, that brought agayne from deeth our Lord Jesus, the greate Shepeherd of the shepe, through the bloudd of the euerlastyng testament, make you perfect in all good worckes to do his wyll, worckyng in you that which is perfect in his syght, onely throughe

GOD GRANT YOU GRACE TO REPENT.

praying God, your olde idolatrye, fornycacyon, and aduouterye, from persecutynge Christe in his sayntes, from your inordynate couetuousnes, and from your euell suppressynge of the pore. And geue you grace, that, nowe at the laste, ye maye repent and beleue the Gospell in embrasynge the same, sekynge Godes glorye onelye, and the commone welth, as in tymes paste ye haue done your owne; and dylygentlye to prouyde for the pore, whyche aboue all other thynges shalbe demaunded of you at the greate daye of the Lorde, as afore is sayde.

that you may repent and believe,

and provide for the poor.

If you do thus, God will have mercy on you.

And thus doynge, doubt not but the plages which ye haue ryghtfullye deserued, God, of his bottomelesse mercye, will turne them from you, as he dede by the Niniuites, whyche repented when they ware warned by Ionas the Prophete. Yf not, loke for no lesse plages then[1] Ierusalem and other Cityes had for their inyquytye.[2]

Awake and turn to the Lord.

Awake, therfore, and repent and turne to the Lorde yet in tyme, and he wyll turne to you. That graunt the Lorde of all lordes and Father of mercye. Amen.

The grace of God[3] (through our Lorde Iesus Christ) be wyth you all.

¶[4] Prynted at Nurenbergh in the yeare
of our Lorde .M D X L V. in
the laste of Nouembre.

[Bodleian Press-mark: Crynes 872. (2).]

---

[1] A came to, *after* then

[2] A *has, after* inyquytye :
And thoughe this be wrytten by a synfull man, yet take it for no lesse than a warnyng, and not to be myne Acte but Gods. For it is not a mannes act to put his lyfe in Ieopardie to call his brethern to the knowdlege of the gospel without a worldly profyt, as this can be none to me. Bewarre therfore I saye, and amend quyckly, For ye haue, if ye marck it well, bene warned almost this 20 yeares, and that manifestly. And they that refuse the warnyng of the Lorde, neuer eskape most greuouse punnyshment.

[3] A our heuenly Father, *for* God

[4] A *has, instead of the above colophon, as follows:*
Made by Roderigo Mors, and Prynted at Jericho in the Land of Promes. By Thome Trouth.
B *has no colophon.*

NOTES.

NOTES RELATING TO THE FAMILY OF BRINKLOW,

BY COL. J. L. CHESTER.

Robert Brynkelowe had a lease, 22 May, 35 Henry VIII (1543), of a small manor or farm called " Hanfeldis," or " Hamvilds," " Hamfelds," or " Hannville," as it is variously spelt (probably Hanfield or Hamfield) in the parish of Kintbury, co. Berks. His mother was buried in Kintbury Churchyard before 5 June 1543, and his father was then evidently dead also. His will, dated 5 June, with a codicil 19 July, was proved in the Prerogative Court of Canterbury 14 Sep. 1543, and is recorded in the volume named " Spert " at folio 24. From the character of his bequests, it is evident that he was in comfortable circumstances, but it is equally clear that he did not rank among the gentry. He had living at his death the following children, and named in the following order in his will :
 1. Henry.
 2. Joane, then wife of (blank) Crouche, or Croucher.
 3. Agnes, then wife of (blank) Chapperleyn, with daughters Joane and Alice.
 4. John, then unmarried.
 5. Alice, then wife of John Revell.
 6. George, to whom was bequeathed a house and land at Engloode in Kintbury.
 7. Hugh, who was one of his father's executors.
 8. William, to whom was bequeathed a tenement in Chilton, held of the Queen.
 9. Anthony, who was named as one of his father's executors, but renounced the execution of his will.

These children appear to have been by a former wife, of whom nothing is known. He left a wife living, called *Sibell*, in the will, but whose name was evidently Isabell, and she appears to have been the widow of . . . . Butler when he married her. From her will it is probable that she was the mother of Edward Butler, of Reading, whose monumental inscription is given in Ashmole's Berkshire, II. 351, and in Coates's History of Reading, p. 174.

Of Joane, the 2nd child, I find nothing further.

Of Agnes, the 3rd child, I find nothing further, but her daughter, Alice Chapperleyn, is mentioned in Henry Brinklow's will, as living at its date 20 June 1545, unmarried.

Of John, the 4th child, nothing is to be found, except that he was living 20 June 1545—that he married, and that both he and his wife died before 24 July 1574, when their son John made his will, and who evidently died unmarried, leaving a brother, or brothers living.

Of Alice, the 5th child, both she and her husband were living 24 Nov. 1562, when he was a witness to the will of her brother Hugh, and called himself " Surveyor."

Of George, the 6th child, I find only that he was living 20 June 1545.

Hugh, the 7th child, became a Citizen and Mercer of London. His will, dated 24 Nov. 1562, was proved 12 Feb. following. He left a wife Mary, and a daughter Cicely, and a son Thomas, then both minors.

William, the 8th child, was living 20 June 1545.

Anthony, the 9th child, proved his brother Hugh's will 12 Feb. 1562-3.

Henry Brincklowe, who, if the order of the will is correct, was the eldest son and child, made his will 20 June 1545, calling himself Citizen and Mercer of London, and it was proved 24 Nov. 1546, by his relict Margery. He left an only son, John, of whom nothing further is found. He mentions all his brothers in his will, thus perfectly identifying him as the son of Robert Brynklowe of Kintbury.

I have carefully searched the calendars of wills at the Principal Registry of Probate down to the year 1630,[1] and do not again find the name, nor am I able to learn anything more respecting any of the family, except an important fact concerning Margery, the widow of Henry Brincklowe, or, at least, which I suppose concerns her, though there may be a doubt. On the 27 April 1546, one Stephen Vahan [Vaughan] had a Licence, or Dispensation, from the Faculty Office of the Archbishop of Canterbury, to marry "Margery Brinclow, widow," and in his will, dated 16 Dec. 1549, he names his wife Margery, she being his 2nd wife. If it can be ascertained that Henry Brinklowe died any time *before* 27 April 1546, there will be little doubt as to the identity—but, if after that date, then of course this theory fails. This Stephen Vaughan was grandfather (through his 1st wife) of Sir Rowland Vaughan, of St Mary Spittle, Middx., whose sole daughter and heir married Sir Pawlet St John, and was mother of Oliver 2nd Earl of Bolingbroke.

I append hereto full abstracts of the Wills referred to.

[1] See Note, p. 132.

ABSTRACTS OF WILLS RELATING TO THE BRINKLOW FAMILY,

IN THE PREROGATIVE COURT OF CANTERBURY

(Now Her Majesty's Court of Probate).

(24 Spert) *Robert Brynklowe* of Hanfeldis, co. Berks — dated 5 June 1543, to be buried in the Churchyard of Kyntbury beside the body of my mother, if I die in those parts—to Sibell my wife 4 keen and a bull, 2 oxen, 2 geldings, a mare, 3 barrow hogs, 2 sows, a boar, 5 quarters of wheat, 5 quarters of barley, 2 goblets of silver, a salt of silver with a cover, a pot of silver, 8 silver spoons which were hers before I married her, 20 sheep, 3 feather beds, the cupboard in the parlour, 2 folding tables, and such pewter vessels as were hers before I married her, provided that she make no further claim to my estate—to my son *Henry Brynklowe* my great brass pot, my great water chaffer, a brason morter, a salt of silver with a cover, and 40 sheep—to my daughter Johane Crowcher 20 sheep—" *to Henry his Son John Brynklowe*" all my silver spoons—to my daughter Agnes Chapperleyn a feather bed and bolster and 20 sheep, and to her daughters Joane and Alice Chapperleyn each 2 ewes—to my son John Brynklowe the lease of my farm of Hamvilds, on condition that he do not give or sell same, but suffer it to remain to his wife and children ; but if he die before marriage, then the lease to remain to my executors—also to said John 2 bullocks for his plough, a horse or mare, an iron bound cart, a plough, my second brass pot, and all the hangings of my house in Hamfelds— to my daughter Alice Revell a feather bed and 20 sheep—to my son George Brynklowe my estate and term in my house and land at Engloode in Kintbury aforesaid—to my Son Hugh Brynklowe 20 sheep, &c.—to my Son William Brynklowe 20 sheep, a feather bed, &c., and my tenement in Chilton that I hold of the Queen—to my Son Anthony Brynklowe 20 sheep, &c.—residue of personalty to my said Sons Hugh and Anthony and appoint them executors.—Overseers said *Henry* Brynklowe and Steven Waas.

Codicil, 19 July 1543, revokes bequest of 40 sheep to said *Henry Brynkelowe* and gives him only 20—revokes the bequest of 20 sheep each to said Joane *Crowche* and Alice Revell, and gives the whole sixty to his wife—to *Julian Butler* 10 sheep.

Witnesses, Edward Darell, Esq., Martin Hollond, Vicar of Kintbury, and others.

Proved 14 Sep. 1543, by said Son Hugh Brinklowe, power being reserved to said Son Anthony.

(38 Pyuning) *Isabell Brynklowe*, of Redyng, widow—dated 29 July 1545—to be buried in St Lawrence Church—to Joane my daughter my household stuff and £20 that my Son Edward Butler hath in his hands.

Letters of administration granted 23 Oct. 1545 to Christopher Butler, son of deceased.

(20 Alen) *Henry Brincklowe*, Citizen and Mercer of London—dated 20 June 1545—I appoint my wife Margery executrix—my goods into 3 parts, according to the custom of London, of which one to my said wife and one to my son John, or, if my wife be with child, same to be divided equally between them when of full age, but if both die before, then their portion to be divided into 2 parts, of which one to my wife, and one equally among all my brethren, viz. John, George, Hugh, William, and Anthony—my brothers Hugh and Anthony to have the care of my child's or children's part till they be of lawful age—out of my 3rd part, as follows:—to my brother Hugh my second bed, bedstead, &c., and my best furred gown—to my brother Anthony £20—to my brother John £4—to my brother George £4—to my brother William £10—to Rose Hasarde £10 at her marriage—to Joyce Copleston £10 at her marriage—to Alice Chaperleyn £10 at marriage, but, if she die before, same to be given to 10 of the poorest householders in Kynbery and Kynbery parish in co. Berks—to Jeffery Dokatt my servant £6 13 4—to Thomas Carrell my servant 40s.—to my cousin Elizabeth Crakingthorpe a ring of 13s. 4d. value, and like rings to my cousin Margery Strong, my sister Masy, my sister Mychill and my sister Brodley [probably his wife's sisters]—to the poor £30 [equal to £300 or £400 at the present day, if not more]—to the godly learned men which labour in the Vineyard of the Lord &c. and fight against Antichrist, £5—for a dinner for my neighbours at my burial £5—I forbid mourning gowns to be worn for me, nor no multitude of torches and tapers &c.—residue of personalty to Margery my wife, on condition that she wear no worldly fantastical dissembling black gown for me, &c. "I will my hole creditt be paide althoughe bothe my wiffe and my children be lefte very pore"—appoint my brothers Hugh and Anthony overseers. Proved 24 Nov. 1546 by the relict Margery.

(9 Chayre) *Hugh Brynckelowe*, Citizen and Mercer of London—dated 24 Nov. 1562—my goods into 3 parts &c.—one to Mary my wife, and one to my 2 children Cycely and Thomas equally—to said 2 children each £10, and if either die before of full age or marriage the other to have both sums—to Margett Bryncklowe my maid £3 6 8—to Jacobe Brynkelowe my brother's servant 40s.—to the poor of St Laurence Jewry 40s.—to my brother Anthony Brynkelowe and my brother-in-law John Revell and my sister his wife each a ring of 40s.—to the poor of Christ's Hospital 40s.—residue to my wife Mary and appoint her executrix—overseers my brother Anthony Brynckelowe and my brother John Revell — witnesses, John Revell, Surveyor, and others. Letters of Administration granted 12 Feb. 1562-3, to Anthony Bryncklowe brother of deceased, the relict Mary renouncing.

(10 Tyrwhit) *John Brincklowe*, of London, one of the Sons of John Brincklowe while he lived of Kemberye co. Berks, dated 24 July 1574—to my cousins Edward and William Penney £6 in the hands of my uncle Edward Butler—to my said uncle Edward Butler all my estate in the farm of Hamville co. Berks, the lease of which beareth date 22

May 35 Henry VIII. (1543) and which I ought to have by virtue of the last will and testament of said John Brinckelowe my father—residue to my said uncle Edward Butler, and appoint him executor.

Proved 16 Feb. 1581-2 by the executor, under a Sentence Definitive, after proceedings between him and Robert Brincklowe.

JOSEPH L. CHESTER, COL.

The Rising in the North, pp. 16, 53, 117.—For a reference to one outbreak, see Notes to *Four Supplications*, p. 103. For the rising known as the Pilgrimage of Grace consult *Froude*, iii. chap. xiii. p. 86 et seq. (1858). See also *Chronicle of the Grey Friars*, pp. 38, 39. *Holinshed's Chron.* iii. fol. 941 (ed. 1587) has the following : It was bruited " abroad that the king pretended to have the gold in the hands of his subjects brought into the Tower to be touched, and all their cattle unmarked, the chalices, goods, and ornaments of parish churches, fines for christenings, weddings and buryings, licences to eat white meat, bread, pig, goose or capon, with many other slanderous, false and detestable tales and lies, forged of devilish purpose to encourage the people to rebellion."

On fol. 942 the Chronicle continues : " After the Lincolnshire rising Yorkshire came. These men declared by proclamation that this their rising and commotion should extend no further, but only to the maintenance and defence of the faith of Christ and deliverance of holy church now decayed and oppressed, and also for the furtherance as well of private as public matters in the realm, touching the wealth of all the king's poor subjects." Further on, fol. 953, we read of another rebellion begun in Yorkshire by five priests and others. To these may be added the following :—

" And in September [1536] after was a rysynge in Lyngcolshere of the comons for taske and talenge of ane abbé there, by the menys of lorde Darcy, lord Husey, sir Robert Constabull, and Roberte Aske. And the vij. day of October the duke of Norffoke and the duke of Suffoke went thither and pacified them ; and then beganne Yorkechere to ryse and they pacifyed them the xxix day of October."—*Grey Friar's Chron.* pp. 38, 39.

Royal Purveyors, p. 19.—In Queen Elizabeth's time Her Majesty's purveyors paid at Faversham, 6s. 8d. a quarter for wheat when the price averaged £1. 6. 4 a quarter. See my paper on *Some Tudor Prices in Kent*, Trans. of the R. Historical Soc., vol. i.

Augmentations, Court of (p. 24) : Established 1536, to take cognizance of all matters concerning the revenue arising from the suppressed monasteries. The Court consisted of a chancellor, treasurer, attorney, and solicitor, ten auditors, seventeen receivers, a clerk, an usher, and a messenger (Rapin, i. 809, and note 2).—Thomas's *Historical Notes.*

Richard Rich, afterwards infamous as Lord High Chancellor of

England, was the first chancellor of the Augmentation Court. See *Chron. Grey Friars*, p. 39.

Abuses in the Law, p. 25. The following is taken from the *Times* of October 31, 1874.

FOURTH COURT.

(*Before Mr Commissioner* KERR.)

"For upwards of an hour after the opening of the Court, although there were four cases on the list for trial, the business was at a perfect stand-still, owing to the absence in one of the three other Courts, which were sitting simultaneously, of one or more of the learned counsel, who were instructed either to prosecute or defend the prisoners.

"Mr Commissioner KERR observed that it might be thought degrading to take a leaf out of the book of Scotch law, but the high court of Justiciary in Edinburgh sat every Monday throughout the year for the trial of criminal cases, and as there was consequently no accumulation or congestion of business, the Court invariably got through its work early in the day. In London, however, there were but 12 sessions in the year, each of which as a rule, with four Courts sitting, occupied the greater part of a week. The result was that the same counsel were engaged in most of the cases, and that a number of separate juries had to be kept kicking their heels about day after day. Perhaps it might be as well in future for the counsel to arrange among themselves when the sessions should be held, and then to bring down the Judges and juries after they had completely made up their minds on the point. (A laugh.) He thought the disreputable practice of counsel who were instructed in cases handing their briefs over to others who knew nothing of the facts should be discountenanced and stopped. Sir Cresswell Cresswell, an eminent counsel and Judge, prided himself that in the whole course of his professional career he had never handed over any brief intrusted to him, and it would be well if Sir Cresswell's high-minded and honourable conduct in that respect could be generally followed. The system at that Court, by which a few counsel monopolized the whole of the business, and then handed over their briefs to juniors if it was inconvenient for them personally to attend to them, was simply detestable. He should like to see every prisoner insist upon being defended by the counsel whom he had instructed and paid, and by no other, and he for one would listen to any application by prisoners to postpone their trials until their own counsel could attend. He believed if he had his own way in that Court for three or four months, he should be able to put things in something like order. The learned Judge, following up these observations, postponed until next Sessions a case, in which the defendant was out on bail, where his counsel was then engaged in another court and could not represent him. In another case a prisoner said his wife had instructed a barrister, whom he named, to defend him, but he now found that the same counsel was conducting the prosecution against him. Mr Commissioner Kerr said there must be some mistake, for, bad as things undoubtedly were, he could not believe that the same counsel would undertake to defend and prosecute the same man. It was then explained that the learned counsel in question, finding that he was instructed for the prosecution, at once returned a brief for the defence which was placed in his hands. The prisoner inquired if the money which his wife had paid was lost to him. Mr Commissioner Kerr said he hoped not, but it all depended upon certain professional rules of etiquette, into which he could not then enter. A barrister present said it depended, in addition, upon the common honesty of the counsel. Mr Commissioner Kerr remarked that that was a long since exploded doctrine, for the fee given to counsel was merely an *honorarium*. With that the business of the Court was proceeded with."

The Murder in the Bishop of Winchester's lodge (p. 29) has eluded my search : it may have been no more than a case of suspicion, as it was common to attribute to violence such deaths as occurred in prison, especially if the deceased were under confinement for political or religious offences.

Hunne, p. 29.—For Hunne's case, the reader is referred to Mr Furnivall's Notes to Fish's *Supplicacyon for the Beggers*, p. 16.

Moore, p. 30.—I do not understand this reference : If any heretic of this name bore a faggot of rushes privately, I have failed to trace him. If it refers to any act of Sir T. More, during his Chancellorship, I cannot find the particular case. Foxe brings several charges of punishment inflicted in his garden against him, and Lord Campbell (*Lives of the Lord Chancellors*, i. 546, ed. 1845) mentions some other cases which More explained. I am inclined to think that some obscure individual named Moóre was subjected to this mild form of punishment, but that the story was not thought much of.

Shooter's Hill, Newmarket Heath, and Stangate Hole (p. 40).—The names of Shooter's Hill and Newmarket Heath are well known. Stangate Hole probably refers to Stangate which was in Lambeth, at the foot of Westminster Bridge, a little above the Bridge and facing the Houses of Parliament. In Latimer's Third Sermon, preached before Edward VI. (Parker Society, Latimer's Sermons, vol. i. p. 139), is the following. He is speaking of Isaiah reproving the magistrates.

" Was he worthy to live in a commonwealth that would call princes on this wise, fellows of thieves ? Had they a standing at *Shooter's Hill*, or *Standgate Hole*, to take a purse ? " [And a foot-note to this says these well-known localities were formerly noted for robberies.] There is, or was, a Stangate Creek in the Isle of Sheppy.

Barnes, Garret, and Jerome, pp. 31, 56.—Also this same yere [1527] doctor Barnes the Austyne freer, two Esterlynges, and two other men shulde a stonde at Powlles crosse at the sermonde with faggottes and tapers, but for because of rayne they stode on the hye scaffolde within the church, and the byshoppe of Rochester Fycher dyd preche; this was the xvj. day of February, and then Barnes was delyueryd home to prisone, but he brake awaye from them and went beyend see unto Luter.—*Chron. Grey Friars of London*, p. 33.

Also this same yere [1540] at sent Mary spettell, the iij. dayes in Ester weke, preched the vicar of Stepney one Jerome; doctor Barnes the ij^{de} daye; and the iij^{de} Garrard passone of Honylane, and there recantyd and askyd the pepulle foryefnes for that they had preched before contrary to the lawe of God. And doctor Barnes, that was the Austyn freer, askyd there the byshoppe of Wenchester foryefnes opynly, and prayd hym yf he wolde foryeffe hym that he wolde make some tokyne and holde up hys honde.—*Id.* p. 43. Barnes asked forgiveness of the Bishop of Winchester, Stephen Gardiner, in vain. The Bishop gave no sign of mercy, and all three went to Smithfield on the 30th day of June, 1540.

On the very day that these three suffered death by burning for the Gospel, three others, Powel, Featherstone, and Abel, were hanged for popery!—*Foxe*, 8vo. v. 439. But see *Froude*, iii. 526, ed. 1858.

Translation of the Bible, p. 54.—Taverner's Bible appeared in 1539. See Notes to the *Supplications*, p. 104. Matthewe's Bible appeared "about 1537," says Foxe. Tyndale and Miles Coverdale made the translation, but as the name of Tyndale was then "odious," it was thought better to father it by a strange name of Thomas Matthew (*Foxe*, 8vo. v. 410); and the same version, after revision, was reprinted in 1538, 1539, 1540, and 1541.—*Froude, Eng. Hist.*, iv. 289, ed. 1858.

Porter, p. 54.—For an account of Porter's martyrdom in 1541, for reading the Bible in St Paul's, see *Foxe*, 8vo. v. 451.

John Tewksbury (p. 56), leatherseller of the parish of St Michael the Quern, London, brought up before Sir T. More, cruelly treated, and burned in Smithfield Dec. 1531. *Strype's Memorials*, vol. i. part I. p. 315; *Foxe's Acts and Monuments* (ed. 1846), vol. iv. pp. 688—694.

James Bainham (p. 56), gentleman and lawyer of the Middle Temple, tortured, and burned at Smithfield 30 April, 1532. *Foxe, Acts*, vol. iv. pp. 697—704; *Strype, Mem.*, vol. i. part I. 315.

John Frith, p. 56, was burnt in Smithfield in 1533. The whole story is contained in *Foxe*, v. 1—16 (8vo.). The Book against the Sacrament was prohibited by the King (*Ib.* v. 567) and answered by Sir Thomas More. The "sum" of the book is given by *Foxe*, v. 7.

Bilney (p. 56) was burnt at Norwich in 1531. *Foxe*, iv. 655. See *Froude*, ii. 83—85, ed. 1856.

Tyndale (p. 56) was burnt by the Emperor's decree at the town of Filford, about 18 miles from Antwerp, in 1536. See the whole story in Foxe. Also see *Froude, Hist. Eng.*, iii. pp. 84, 85, ed. 1858.

The Bishop of Winchester at Ratisbon (pp. 58, 61).—"About the year 1538 a diet was held at Ratisbone [Latin Regenspurg], whither

King Henry sent Bishop Gardiner and Sir Henry Knevit his joint ambassadors: where also was Contarini a legate from the Pope. This legate brought letters from the Pope to Winchester; and going away suddenly, desired an Italian merchant, named Lodovico, to go to Winchester, and to hasten his answer to the Pope's pacquet; for that the carrier was ready to depart in a day or two. This Lodovico soon after meeting one Wolf, steward to Sir H. Knevit, prayed him that he would tell the English ambassador what the legate desired. Wolf told him there were two ambassadors and asked him 'which?' He said he 'knew not that,' but he said it was a bishop, whom he styled reverendissimo. This Wolf discovered to Mr Chaloner, Sir H. Knevit's secretary, and him Wolf carried to Lodovico, that there might be another witness besides himself; and there pumped him so in Chaloner's company, that he again spake of it. This whole matter was fully related by these two persons to Knevit, and he sent notice of it to the King. The King thought fit at that time to put it up; and sent word to Knevit and the Bishop (who had words together about this) that they should both unite and mind his business."—From *Strype's Memorials*, vol. iii. part I. p. 456. Lodovico seems to have been put in prison, and the Bishop referred the matter to the Emperor's minister Granvela, who was a great friend to the Pope. Dr Fulke's Defence of the English Translations of the Bible, Parker Society, p. 489, speaking of the King's title of "Supreme head," adds—

"But as *Stephen Gardiner* understood that title in conference with Bucer at *Ratisbon*, we do utterly abhor it, and so did all godly men always, that a king should have absolute power to do in religion what he will."

The Marquis of Exeter (p. 58) and de la Pole, Lord Montague, were cousins to the King, who wished to condemn them for high treason on a charge of corresponding with Cardinal Pole. Baron Audley presided as High Steward, and, as it was the Royal wish, of course they were condemned and executed. See *Lord Campbell's Lives of the Lord Chancellors*, i. 608, ed. 1845.

Calling on the Virgin Mary for help, p. 60.—On the 22nd of August, 1874, an attempt was made to assassinate the President of the Republic of Peru. *La Patria* (Lima) of the 10th of October following contained the following notice:—

"FIESTAS RELIGIOSAS.—Mañana se celebran las siguientes:

"En la Merced, misa de gracias á la Vírjen por la salvacion de la vida de S. E. el presidente de la república del atentado del 22 de agosto último.

"En Santo Domingo la fiesta de nuestra Sra. del Rosario, á las once del dia, y procesion de la imágen á la plaza de armas, á las cuatro.

"Una banda de música acompañará á la procesion en su paseo."

"RELIGIOUS FEASTS.—To-morrow will be celebrated the following: In the (church of) The Mercea, a thanksgiving Mass to the Virgin for the salvation of the life of His Excellency the President of the Republic from the attempt of the 22nd of August last.

"In Santo Domingo the Feast of Our Lady of the Rosary at eleven o'clock in the morning, and a procession of the Image to the Plaza de Armas at four o'clock. A band of music will accompany the procession on its way."

The Feast in Santo Domingo had nothing to do with the object of the Mass at the Mercea. The Church of Santo Domingo is rich in the possession of a Bead which (it is said) belonged to the Rosary of the Virgin.

The Church of St Mary Overys, p. 61.—About Christmas, 1540, the priory church of St Mary Overies, Southwark, was purchased of the King by the inhabitants of the Borough, Dr Gardiner, Bishop of Winchester, lending a helping hand. It was made with the adjoining little church of Mary Magdalene into a parish church. *Holinshed*, fol. 950, ed. 1587. It is now better known as St Saviour's, Southwark

The Bishop of Winchester and Images (p. 61).—Gardiner was considered to be a great favourer of images, and he used arguments against their destruction, which are quoted by Latimer in his sermon of the Plow. In the beginning of the reign of Hen. VIII. "the people were very forward in pulling down and defacing images, even without permission. This was done in Portsmouth, where divers crucifixes and Saints were plucked down and destroyed." Gardiner wrote to the Captain of Portsmouth and the Mayor, and even went there himself to find who had done it. He said, "that such as were affected with this principle of breaking down images, were hogs, and worse than hogs, and were ever so taken in England, being called Lollards. And that the maintenance of this opinion of destroying images was utterly disliked in Germany: and such men were counted the dregs cast out by Luther, after all his brewings of Christ's religion. And he [Bishop Gardiner] himself had seen images standing in all their churches."—*Strype's Memorials*, vol. ii. part I. p. 54.

Cole (pp. 61, 62).—There were several Coles of whom scattered notices are given by Strype. It is probable that Henry Cole, Warden of New College, Oxford, afterwards one of the Commissioners for the restitution of Bonner, was the man referred to; the same man appears to have been used by Pole also. His connection with Gardiner seems obscure. But see the Works of Bishop Jewel, 1st Portion (Parker Society), p. 60. This volume contains the Controversy of Dr Henry Cole with Jewel; a side-note to some remarks on the book *De Vera Obedientia*, and its approvers, says that these were "Gardiner, Bonner, Tunstall, Doctor Cole, and almost all the rest," as though they were all of one side.

Marriage Laws, p. 64.—See *Tudor Ballads*, p. 477, for the alacrity with which some of the Reformers put away their wives. Even Cranmer sent his wife with all quietness back to Germany.

Bishops as Ambassadors, p. 69.—The Bishop of Winchester went as

Ambassador to France in October, 1535, and remained three years. *Holinshed's Chron.* iii. 939, ed. 1587. Bonner, Bishop of London, was Ambassador resident in France in 1538. *Foxe*, v. 150 (8vo.). The *Index* to Froude's Eng. Hist. may be consulted by the reader, but I apprehend with little satisfaction to himself and with many mental maledictions on its compiler. Taking the first seven references under the word "Bonner," I found them all useless. I used the copy in the Reading Room, British Museum. The *Index* to the 8vo. ed. of *Foxe* is not much better.

The Parliaments of 1541, p. 70.—The 16th of January, 1542, began a parliament, says Holinshed, vol. iii. fol. 955, but I suppose he and Brinklow refer to the same parliament.

Warnmall Quest, p. 91.—It seems very probable that this is only another term for, or corruption of, *Wardmote Quest.* Among the articles of the charge of the Wardmote inquest were the following: " You shall truly inquire if any person keep any bawdy house, gaming house, or other house of ill fame." *Pulling on the Laws, Custom, &c., of the City and Port of London*, p. 219, *note*, ed. 1842. See also a process of Inquisition, &c., made in 1311, *Memorials of London*, &c., by H. J. Riley, M.A., p. 86, ed. 1868.

Soper Lane, p. 100, was on the site of the present Queen Street, Cheapside. It took its name from the Soapers or Soap-makers. In 1297 a serious riot occurred there at a market held after dinner, and the market, which had been established by strangers, foreigners, and beggars, was abolished. The Pepperers, or Spicers, inhabited it in the reign of Edward II.; then, some seventy years later, the Curriers and Cord-wainers had possession; and in Henry's time, as we see, the Pie-makers had it. See *Riley's Memorials of London*, p. 33.

Pardons sold in Lombard Street, p. 100.—Lombard Street in Brinklow's time, as well as before and after, might almost have been called the Market Place of London. He who had anything to sell, or anything on which he could borrow money, went there; and there he would be sure to encounter some one who had come thither to buy or who had money which he wished to lend. Among others would be the vendor of pardons, of relics, or of images, " and other of their tromperye," who, between Englishmen and foreigners, would probably drive a fair trade.

Master Standish (p. 102).—There were several men of the name of Standish. Henry Standish, the enemy of Dean Colet, was Bishop of St Asaph from 1515 to 1536 A.D. A Dr Standish, perhaps the same man, wrote in 1554 a book against the printing of the Scriptures in English— " A Discourse wherein is debated, whether it be expedient that the Scripture should be in English, for all men to read that will." Fulke's Defence, &c. (Parker Society), Epist. Dedicatory, p. 4, *note*, says, John Standish was admitted a probationer fellow of Corpus Christi, Oxford, in 1528. In the time of Edward VI. he was a zealous reformer, made rector of Wigan, and married; but was separated from his wife when Queen Mary ascended the throne, and deprived of his preferment.

Bishop Bonner, for his affections to Popery, gave him the rectory of Packlesham. Among other works he wrote " A Treatise against the translation of the Bible into the vulgar tongue." *Wood's Athenæ*, vol. i. p. 236-8.

Bale's Select Works (Parker Society), p. 172 (the First Examination of Mistress Anne Askew). [Anne Askew says how Dr Standish tempted her to speak as to a text of St Paul's.[1] John Bale replies] " It is not yet half a score of years ago, since this blasphemous idiot Standish compared, in a lewd sermon of his, the dear price of our redemption, or precious blood of Christ, to the blood of a filthy swine, like himself a swine."

King John and Stephen Langton, pp. 107, 108.—I have before remarked that the church has often had the courage to protest against the oppressions of the strong, and that it has been fortunate for us as a nation that the abject submission taught by the Reformers has not been common among our religious teachers.[2] The following quotation will not be out of place here. " During the Middle Ages, heresy was often extinguished in blood, but in every Cisalpine country a principle of liberty, to a great extent, held its own, and national life refused to be put down. Nay more, these precious and inestimable gifts had not infrequently for their champions a local prelacy and clergy. The Constitutions of Clarendon, cursed from the Papal throne, had the support of the English Bishops. Stephen Langton, appointed directly, through an extraordinary stretch of power, by Innocent III., to the See of Canterbury, headed the Barons of England in extorting from the Papal minion John, the worst and basest of all our Sovereigns, that Magna Charta, which the Pope at once visited with his anathemas. In the reign of Henry VIII., it was Tunstal, Bishop of Durham, who first wrote against the Papal domination. Tunstal was followed by Gardiner; and even the recognition of the Royal Headship was voted by the clergy, not under Cranmer, but under his unsuspected predecessor Warham. Strong and domineering as was the high Papal party in these centuries, the resistance was manful."—*The Vatican Decrees, &c.*, *by the Rt Hon. W. E. Gladstone, M.P.*, pp. 26, 27.

Winchester's Garden (p. 110).—Probably a reference to a bit of contemporary scandal which concerns us very little to know. But see p. 64.

The Brinklow Family, p. 122. Mr H. E. Barnes of Mercers' Hall has most kindly examined the Books of the Mercers' Company for me. He finds that in 1541 Hugh Brinklow was an apprentice to Henry Brinklow, and that in 1545 Anthony was an apprentice to Henry. These two apprentices seem to have been the younger brothers of Henry, mentioned by Col. Chester on p. 121. In 1582 the name of Anthony Brinklow, son of Anthony, occurs, and in 1609 Robert, the son of Anthony, is mentioned. The name does not occur again.

[1] This was in 1545.   [2] See Crowley's Works, Introduction, xxi.

GLOSSARIAL INDEX.

ADVOUTERYE, p. 120, adultery.

Angles, p. 97, angels.

Bald, a bald reason, p. 15, a useless, unprofitable reason.

Batel, batel ground, p. 16, fruitful or fertile ground.

Bayght, p. 24, bait.

Bearewolfe, pp. 110, 112, a roaring wolf, a devouring brute; probably the same as were-wolf, a man-wolf.

Belly goddys, p. 52, people whose god is their belly.

Berewolues, p. 89, 94. *See* Bearewolfe.

Blearynge, p. 99, blearing the eyes, blinding the eyes, befooling.

Blessing, the Bishops', pp. 56, 105, a phrase applied to the punishment bestowed upon heretics.

Bowget, p. 45, a bouget, budget, or portmanteau.

Boytrye, p. 26.

Bussardys, p. 52. Bussard, a great drinker.

Buzarde, p. 111, a blockhead, a dunce.—*Ascham.* A moth or beetle that flies by night, "as blind as a buzzard." (*Halliwell* and *Nares*.)

Bydores, p. 94, secret doors: or an irregular entrance.

Bytch, bitch, p. 63. *See* Sawt.

Card, brag it owt with a carde of x, p. 43. Nares says, "To *face it with a card of ten;* a common phrase, which we may suppose to have been derived from some game (possibly *primero*) wherein the standing boldly upon a *ten* was often successful. A *card of ten* meant a tenth card, a ten . . . .
Some may be *coats*, as in the cards: but then
Some must be knaves, some varlets, bawds, and ostlers,
As aces, duces, *cards o' ten to face it*
Out, i' the game which all the world is.—*B. Jons., New Inn,* i. 3.
Skelton is also quoted for the expression,
First pycke a quarrel, and fall out with him then,
And so *out face him with a card of ten.*
I conceive the force of the phrase to have expressed originally the confidence or importance of one who, with a ten, as at brag, *faced*, or *outfaced* one who had really a faced card against him."

Carl, p. 9, churl.

Carsey, p. 12, kersey.

Cast, p. 87, custom, device.

Channsynge, p. 113, chancing.

Chepe, better chepe, p. 11, better bargain, cheaper.

134 GLOSSARIAL INDEX.

Contynent, in contynent, p. 111, incontinent, without delay.

Coragyng, p. 22, encouraging.

Cracker, a ioly cracker, p. 13, a boaster.

Deale, part; " after deale and fore deale," p. 41.

Differ, p. 114, defer.

Domme, p. 104, dumb.

Eye, (phr.) black is their eye, p. 109, tint of colour: see *Nares*.

Face, to abhor the name of the Pope for a *face*, p. 57.

Foredeale, 41. *See* Deale, forepart.

Founte, p. 100, font.

Gaddinge. *A gaddynge*, p. 82, 83.
To Walsyngham *a gaddyng*,
To Cantorbury a maddyng,
As men distraught of mynde.
Foxe (8vo.), v. 405.

Gere (matter, business), to wink at this gere, p. 92, to let an ill act or custom pass without punishment or reproof.

Grope, p. 112, to search into, or examine.

Grosser, p. 11, engrosser.

Grynnys, p. 31, gins, traps.

Hard, p. 7, heard.

Imbryng Dayes, p. 67. Ember days.

Impropryd, p. 32, impropriated.

Impys, p. 9, imps.

Ipocryte, p. 100, hypocrite.

Knowledge, p. 7, acknowledge.

Leperye, p. 113, leprosy.

Lorel, p. 52. A boor, a low fellow, a clown; *adj.* boorish, low, clownish. See *Prompt. Parvulorum*.

Lubbars, lusty, p. 88, idle fellows.

Lyplabor, p. 67, talk; " my fruitlesse and worthy *lip-labour*."—Taylor's *Workes*, 1630, in Nares.

Lytterynge, p. 117, littering, the act of bringing forth.

Make, p. 117, mate.

Malygnant, p. 116, the Church malignant.

Mase, p. 106, maze.

Massynge, p. 105, saying mass.

Maundaye, p. 102, commandment, ordinance. Lat. *mandatum*.

Meale, peany, p. 88. *See* Peany meale.

Mollifye, p. 91, mollify, soften.

Mommers, p. 70, mummers.

Moory ground, p. 17, moors.

Mynsed, p. 8, minced, affected, as in a minced gait (the word may be a misprint for mysused: see note 1, foot of same p.).

Nede, p. 63, needful or necessary.

Nosel, to *nosel* the peple in idolatry, p. 71, to encourage, to set them on.

Ouerplus, p. 86, more than is wanted.

Oueryocked, p. 73, over yoked, over laden.

Partye, p. 27, person.

Passe, p. 79, to occupy one's self with, to heed.

Patche, p. 85, to add to.

Peany meale, p. 88, penny meal, by pence. See *Four Supplications*, under the word *warmoll*.

Pistels, p. 71, epistles.

Pock in wine and clothes, p. 37, a mark, as in the small-pox: an infection.

Pollagys, p. 55, pollings, taxes, plunderings.

Pricksong, p. 7, music written down, sometimes more particularly in parts; from the points or dots with which it is noted down .... When opposed to *plainsong*, it meant counterpoint as distinguished from melody.—*Nares.*

Pyedly, p. 70, with several colours.

Pyping, p. 8, piping, playing on wind instruments.

Pyty, p. 106, petty.

Pytye (verb), p. 108, to distress, to grieve.

Queane, p. 85. Qy. Is Brinklow punning on the word queen? Elsewhere he writes it quene. Queane, as is well known, will bear another signification.

Rabbles, p. 105, idle, silly, talk.

Raynes, p. 99, cloth of Rennes (?).

Resayued, p. 102, received.

Reygned, p. 18, arraigned.

Rightwysnesse, p. 97, righteousness.

Sawt, a *sawt* bytch, p. 63, salt bitch, lecherous.

Schone, Schone Mary, p. 61, schön, beautiful (German).

Selye, p. 118, simple, innocent.

Seniours, p. 80, seniors, elders.

Snafful, p. 27, snaffle.

Sprete, p. 104, } spirit.
Spryte, p. 98, }

Stone, touch stone, p. 74.

Storyes, p. 117, histories.

Stroke, p. 7, power or influence.

Stoue, p. 43. The poorest may come into their hall or *stoue*, thei being at dynar. A stove, i. e. a confined place, not open but stived-up.

Thynne woddes, p. 99; *thyine* woods, in Rev. xviii. 12, A. Vers., meaning sweet, or sweet-scented woods.

Trishtrash, p. 99, nonsense.

Tromperye, p. 100, trumpery.

Tryshtrash, id.
He that minds *trish-trash*,
Him I will belishbash.
1602. *How a Man may chuse a good Wife.* (Wheatley.)

Valoure, p. 85, value.

Vent, p. 11, sale.

Vyperos, p. 57, cruel, having the nature or qualities of a viper.

Waretack, p. 86, 88, a safeguard: from *ware*, wary, wise, and *tack*, hold, confidence.

Warnmall quest, p. 91. Probably wardmote. See Note, p. 9, vol. of *Supplications* of this Series; also *warmol* in the Glossary to the same volume. Also the Note on p. 131 of this volume.

Wrythers, p. 114, persons who twist or distort words from their natural use or sense, wresting them.

Ynyon, p. 113, phr. To lay, &c., onion.

Yockyd, ouer yockyd, over yoked, p. 5, over laden.

Yockys, p. 6, yokes.

GENERAL INDEX.

ABBEY lands bestowed by the king, 34.
Abbey lands better administered by monks, 9.
Abbey lands, why bestowed originally, 33.
Abbots, causers of troubles as well as bishops, 108.
Absolution useless, 111.
Abundance, the, we have had, 75.
Accusations, wrongful, 21, 22.
Aldermen imprison the poor, 28.
Ambrose, St, referred to, 64.
Anabaptist, I shall be said to be an, 118.
Antichrists, proofs that bishops are, 59.
Apostles, the, refused to be worshipped, 83.
Augmentation, the court of, 24, 125.
Austin, St, quoted on the Lord's Supper, 98.
Authority abused by those who have it, 45.
Bainham, James, Martyr, 56, 128.
Barnes's case referred to, 31, 56, 127.
Barnes burnt because he advocated the cause of the poor, 91.
Becket, Thomas, referred to, 82.

Becket's conduct to King Henry II., 107.
Benefice, a priest ought to have one only, xx, 48.
Bible in English, we have the, 91, 128.
Bible, objections to the translation of, 54, 128.
Bible, the, blasphemed, 54.
Bible, the, refused by the citizens of London, 79.
Bilney and others referred to, 56, 128.
Bishops, a comparison between St Paul's and ours, 70, 71.
Bishops are made ambassadors, 69, 130; houses of bishops, 69.
Bishops and priests, two degrees in the Church, ought to be no more, 47.
Bishops and rich men in league, 80.
Bishops, butchers, 104.
Bishops can only destroy the body, 103.
Bishops, chantries and colleges, down with 'em, 47.
Bishops, character of, 116.
Bishops do not put men to death for Christ's sake, 106.
Bishops, extortions of, 53.

GENERAL INDEX.

Bishops have prisons; why should they? 29; how their prisoners are treated, 30.

Bishops' property, how to bestow, xv, 50, 51, 116.

Bishops robbed of their pope, 35.

Bishops, the blessing of, a fire, 56, 105.

Bishops, the, put men to death who preach, 109.

Bishops, what they teach, 72.

Bonner and Cole put up an image of John Baptist in St Paul's, 61, 130.

Book, another, by Brinklow, referred to, 91, 114.

Bribery in the courts of justice, 25.

Brinklow, banished, 6, and note.

Brinklow family, references to, 121-5, 132.

Chancery, abuses in, 25.

Chantries, 86.

Chantries condemned, 89.

Churches, how served before and after the reformation, 34.

Cloth, English, its price and markets, 11.

Cloth to be made only in cities and towns, 51.

Cole, a scholar of Pole's, 61, 130.

Colleges and chantries to come down, 47; how to apply their wealth, 47, 48.

Confession, abominable, 111.

Confession, auricular, 46.

Confession cannot be well used, 112.

Confession, object of, 111.

Courts of justice to be open at all times, 42.

Customs are too high, 49; prices have risen 5 per cent., 50.

Dead, provision made for, 81, 86, 88.

Dearness of goods, 13.

Dearth caused by lords, 12.

Debtors' goods, how distributed, 41

Deer, punishment for killing a, 17; where they should be kept, 17.

Doctors for the sick poor, 52.

Enclosures, miseries which come of, 16.

English, service ought to be in, xiii, 47.

England compared to Sodom, 75.

England exhorted to awake and amend, 76.

Exchequer, the court of, 24.

Exeter, Marquis of, 58, 129.

Farmers ejected, 9; better off before, 11.

Farmers to have but one farm, 48; extortions of, 48.

Fast, what a true, is, 67.

Felons, forfeiting of goods of, 14.

First-fruits, law of, confirmed by parliament, 39; much worse now *ib.*; evils of, 40.

Flemish custom to be followed, 50.

Font, death in the, 101.

Frith, Bilney, and other martyrs referred to, 56, 128.

Gardiner, S., Bp of Winchester, his immorality, 64, 132. *See* Winchester.

Garret's case referred to, 31, 127.

Germans, the, held up as an example to us, 48.

Germany administers justice better than we do, 43.

Germany, how heretics are treated in, 31, 32.

Germany, Mass reformed in, 87.

Gladstone, Rt Hon. W. E., quoted, xxi, 132.

Gospel, the, to be preached by the king's injunctions, 109.

Grievances to be redressed by parliament, 74.
Harlots' confessions gladly heard, 65.
Hunne's case mentioned, 29, 70, 127.
Idolatry maintained in London, 79.
Images forbidden, 60; churches full of, 61, 130.
Images, idols, down with 'em! 46.
Jerom's case referred to, 31, 127.
John, King, 107, 108, 132.
John's, St, Wood, reference to foxes in, 55.
Judges to be incorruptible, 43.
Judges to be paid by salary, 22, 43; how to be punished for disobedience, 23.
King advised to plunder bishops, 115.
King, a wicked, not to be resisted, 118.
King, the, bishops desired to have for pope, 35.
King, the, his modesty, 36.
King, the, his rents to be lowered, 10; are raised, 13; to do his duty, 15; his money from abbey lands, 23.
King, the, practises popish ceremonies, 89.
King, the, to receive his portion of church property, 51.
King, the, will do better when his subjects do better, 94.
Laity, the, as bad now as the clergy were in times past, 37.
Lands held by Church of Rome, 32.
Langton, Archbp, how he treated King John, 108, 132.
Law, abuses in, 25, 126.
Laws, obedience to the, 5.

Law suits, how prolonged, 25.
Laws, wicked, not to be obeyed, 119.
Lawyers almost as bad as bishops and priests, 21.
Lawyers and their fees, 23.
Lepers, the ten, referred to, 65, 113.
Lombard Street, pardons sold in, 100, 131.
London, its riches, 90.
London, the bishops of, their infamous character, 93.
London, the guilt of, in murdering Christ's servants, 93, 95, 96.
London, worse than Sodom, 95.
Lords and commons ought to sit together, 8.
Maid of Kent, the, referred to, 82.
Marriage and divorce, 63; marriage forbidden, 64, 130.
Marriage and those who condemn it, 46.
Marriage of priests, 110.
Marshalsea, the, to be abolished, 26.
Mary, image of the Schone, 61.
Mary Overys, church of, 61, 130.
Mary, prayers to the Virgin, 60, 129.
Mass, the, an idol, 98.
Matthew's Bible called in, 54.
Monks, hospitality of the, 33.
More and his faggot of rushes, 30, 127.
Music in churches, evils of, xiii, 7.
Nero, our rulers are all like, 75.
Newgate filled with servants, 28.
Newgate, how prisoners are relieved in, 90.
Newmarket Heath referred to, 40, 127.

Non-resistance, doctrine of, 118.
North, rising in the, 16, 53, 117, 125.
Officers, better, to be chosen, 92.
Obits, 86.
Papa translated into pay, pay, 39.
Parliament, a, at Westminster, 70, 131.
Parliament, classes of men chosen to serve in, 13.
Parliament, privileges of, 44.
Parliament, religious exercises for, 7, 8.
Parliament, the, bewitched by bishops, 57.
Parliament, what is done by, "Well done," 35.
Parsons, lord, all thieves and murderers, 36, 38.
Patching and piecing of Christ, 85, 86.
Perjury goes unpunished and why, 25; how to be punished, 30.
Pole referred to, x *et seq.*, 61.
Poor, houses for the, 52.
Poor in a worse condition than before, 10.
Poor not able to live, 9.
Poor, the, are grievously oppressed, 73.
Poor, the, and fast days, 68.
Poor, the, are punished, but the rich go free, 91, 92.
Poor, the, imprisoned, 28.
Poor, the innumerable, of London, 90.
Poor, the, left unaided, 88, 90, 94.
Poor, the, robbed by the royal purveyors, 19, 20.
Poor were relieved by the monks, 33.
Pope, fasting in honour of the, 67.
Pope, laws of the, to be banished, 58.

Pope, London has burnt those who opposed the, 96.
Pope, the, altered the Lord's Supper, 97.
Pope, the, defended by bishops, 56.
Pope, the, not yet banished, 53, 55.
Porter imprisoned by Bonner, 54, 128.
Poverty of the preachers of the new faith, 72.
Priests ought to marry, 46.
Prayers before the parliament, 7.
Prayers for the dead, vain, 88.
Prayers, how they are and how they ought to be said, 66.
Preachers, dangers to, 115.
Preachers ought not to be put into the hands of their accusers, 29.
Preaching, good, in London, 95.
Prisoners, condition of, 27; are confined years without trial, 28.
Prisons kept by bishops, 29.
Psalters, Our Lady's, 67.
Punishment in store for us, 74.
Purveyors, the king's, wrongs done by, 19, 125.
Queen of heaven, calling upon, 84.
Ratisbon, Bp of Winchester at, 61, 128.
Rebellion how avoided, 15.
Regensperg. *See* Ratisbon.
Religion to be reformed, 45.
Rents are raised by landlords, 9; consequences of, 10, 11.
Rents, the king's, to be reduced, 10.
Repentance, an exhortation to, 95.
Riches not to be abused, 17.
Riches of the city abused, 90.
Rich men come first and are first served, 41.

Sacrament, a sign only, 102, 103.
Saints' days, eves of, 60.
Schools, free, to be founded, 52.
Scripture, citizens exhorted to read the, 96.
Scripture, the, and bishops compared, 59.
Scripture, the, what it teaches, 72.
Selfishness to be put away, 74.
Sermon, length of, and how often before parliament, 8.
Servants go unpaid, 44; evil consequences of the custom, 45.
Servants sent to Newgate, 28.
Shooters' Hill referred to, 40, 127.
Soaper Lane, pies sold in, 100, 131.
Standish, Master, referred to, 102, 131.
Stangate Hole referred to, 40, 127.
Sunday, how to keep, 62; how it is kept, 63.
Temporal power, the, supreme, 59.
Tewkesbury martyred, 56, 128.
Theft, punishment for, 18.
Traitors, children of, are punished, 15.
Tyndale referred to, 56, 128.
Vice in the city, 80, 91.
Victuals, the rating of, 19.
Virgin, calling on the, 60, 129.
Wards, selling in marriage of, 18.
Warnmall quest, 91, 131.
Water, Holy, stinks, 100.
William II., how treated by bishops, 107.
Wills of the Brinklow family, 121.
Winchester, Bp of, a man murdered in his lodge, 29. *See* Gardiner.
Winchester, Bp of, at Ratisbone, 61, 128; his immorality, 64.
Winchester's (Bp of) garden referred to, 110, 132.
Winchester, the Bp of, a leader, 70.
Witnesses, men condemned without seeing, 30.
Wolsey, Cardinal, referred to, 82.
Wool bought by foreigners, 11.
Writs, abuse in serving, 20.

The manufacturer's authorised representative in the EU for product safety is Oxford University Press España S.A. of El Parque Empresarial San Fernando de Henares, Avenida de Castilla, 2 - 28830 Madrid (www.oup.es/en or product.safety@oup.com). OUP España S.A. also acts as importer into Spain of products made by the manufacturer.
Printed and bound by CPI Group (UK) Ltd, Croydon, CR0 4YY

22/04/2026

02094916-0008